GHIA

Ford's carrozzeria

A study of one of Italy's oldest and finest coachbuilders

David Burgess-Wise

OSPREY

Published in 1985 by Osprey Publishing Limited
12–14 Long Acre, London WC2E 9LP
Member company of the George Philip Group

Sole distributors for the USA

Osceola, Wisconsin 54020, USA

British Library Cataloguing in Publication Data

Burgess-Wise, David
    Ghia, Ford's carrozzeria: a study of one of Italy's oldest and
    finest coachbuilders.
    1. Ghia, *Firm*——History
    I. Title
    338.7'62926'0945   HD9710,I84G4/

ISBN 0–85045–625–8

Editor Tim Parker
Design Gwyn Lewis

Printed by BAS Printers Limited, Over Wallop, Hampshire

Contents

Foreword

In November of 1984 I received a semi-final draft of 'The Ghia Book', as it was called, waiting for a press-ready title from my friend and fellow Ford employee David Burgess-Wise. The attached letter from David asked that I write a foreword for the publication. Let me tell you, that's like asking a painting student to scribble a few kind words about the definitive history of fine art. To every automotive designer in the world the city of Turin is a magic place. There is absolutely no other place like it on the face of the earth. Imagine having a group of descendants of Lautrec, Giotto, DaVinci and others of that ilk all painting canvases just for you and your friends to admire in the privacy of your own home. Having Ghia SpA report to me is not that different as an analogy. During my years as a designer with Chrysler in the '50s I worked as an apprentice on details of some of the prototypes in those famous shops on via Agostino de Montefeltro and I remember my first time entering that long, dimly lit 'Metal Room.' Cliché or not, I felt the magic. To have, years later, Ford inform me that I was to become President of the *carrozzeria* was an exciting assignment. Anyone who has a love affair with automobiles and is ever fortunate enough to visit that room will attempt to describe that same emotion. David Burgess-Wise has done a lot better job than I could ever hope to do.

D. F. Kopka
President, Ghia SpA
Vice President, Design
Ford Motor Company
January, 1985

A Ghia craftsman shapes a panel for a prototype. The photograph was taken in the mid-1980s but the skill is timeless

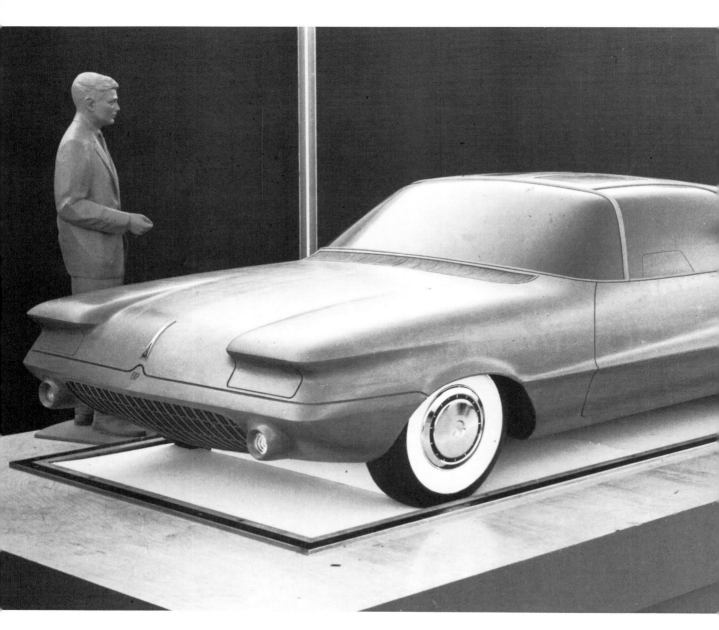

Acknowledgements

This is a book that I wanted to write the first time I visited Ghia in Turin. Nevertheless, a book like this depends on willing help: and that has been forthcoming in generous measure.

So, for their time, trouble, research and reminiscences, I'd like to thank the following friends who made it all possible: Uwe Bahnsen; Petra Billaudelle; Harry Calton; Bill Camplisson; Giles Chapman; Don Kopka; Manfred Lampe; Tom Land; Karl Ludvigsen; Bob Lutz; Giacomo Gaspardo Moro; Dave Rees; Filippo Sapino; Ken Shipton; Herman Smith; Tom Tjaarda and Nino Vaccarella.

The following periodicals, past and present, also provided valuable information: *Autocar, Car, Classic & Sports Car, Custom Car, Eco Motori, Milleruote, Motor, Motor 16, Motor Italia, Motor Trend, Motori Aeri Cicli & Sport, On Four Wheels, Rapiditas, Rivista Fiat, Road Test, Special Interest Autos* and *Torino Motori*.

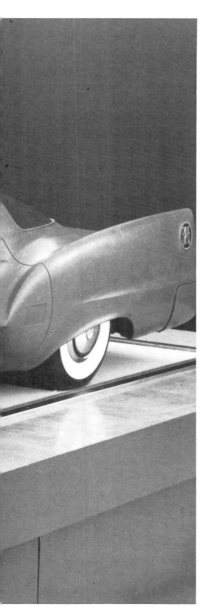

EXP-6, a typically exuberant Virgil Exner design for a Ghia-built Chrysler concept car: the photograph was discovered in the Ghia archives in 1984

Le vetture Diatto della Targa Florio

GAMBONI SU VETTURA DIATTO TIPO 4 DC - 25 HP PER LA TARGA FLORIO.

GHIA SU VETTURA DIATTO TIPO 4 DC - 25 HP PER LA TARGA FLORIO.

1 Signor Ghia takes the wheel

Ghia: it's a name that today is well known all round the world thanks to the use of the Ghia badge on top-of-the-range Ford vehicles and crowd-pulling concept cars for motor shows; but there was a Carrozzeria Ghia in Turin years before the association with Ford, and in its long and colourful history, the company has probably built bespoke bodywork for more makes of car than any other Torinese coachbuilder. Moreover, the man whose name it bears was one of the true, if unsung, pioneers of the Italian motor industry.

Born in Turin on 18 September, 1887, Giacinto Ghia was appreticed at the turn of the century to a small firm of carriage builders; Turin, however, was rapidly establishing itself as the centre of Italy's nascent automobile industry, so it wasn't long before young Giacinto decided that horse-drawn transportation was decidedly passé, and left the little coachworks to enter the new and exciting world of the motor vehicle; according to a postwar survey of Italian coachbuilders, young Ghia spent the next few years in 'a serious and fruitful apprenticeship with various Torinese companies', progressing from mere mechanic to the more exacting job of testing new cars.

Like most of Turin's early motoring history, the Ghia story is linked with one of the many companies promoted by the four Ceirano brothers, in this case the most active of the quartet, Giovanni Battista Ceirano, whose 'Welleyes' voiturette had been the root from which Fiat had sprung, and whose original workforce had included such stars in the ascendant as Vincenzo Lancia and Felice Nazzaro.

Giovanni Battista had resigned from Fiat, (or F.I.A.T. as it was then known, from its full title of Fabbrica Italiana Automobili Torino, the acronym not being adopted until the end of 1906) in 1901, to join his brother Matteo in building Ceirano cars in a factory in the Corso Vittorio Emanuele; despite the services of designers such as Balloco (who later joined Itala) and Faccioli (who started with Welleyes and subsequently went to Fiat, then to SPA), the fraternal venture did not go well, and in 1903 went into liquidation.

Matteo left, and another brother, confusingly named Giovanni, joined Giovanni Battista in a revived company making cars powered by single-cylinder De Dion engines.

This failed even more quickly than its predecessor, and Giovanni left *ben presto* to found the Junior company, while Giovanni Battista, having attracted

Ghia and Gamboni in the Diatto Tipo 4 DC racers built for the 1919 Targa Florio; Ghia's chances of glory were cut short when he swerved to avoid an 'imprudent kid' and crashed on the first lap

CARROZZERIA GHIA & GARIGLIO
COSTRUZIONE SOLIDA - FINIZIONE DI LUSSO - SPECIALITA' TIPI SPORT

Carrozzeria Ghia e Gariglio - Landaulet di serie su chassis Spa modello 23.000

N. 4, CORSO VALENTINO - **TORINO** - CORSO VALENTINO, N. 4

CARROZZERIE di GRAN LUSSO e di GRAN SPORT

Anche nei tipi sport la clientela desidera oggi il comfort e la signorilità. Eccone un modello, che unisce queste qualità a una bella linea sobria e moderna, costruito dalla Carrozzeria GHIA e GARIGLIO di Torino.

Carrozzeria GHIA & GARIGLIO - TORINO
CORSO VALENTINO N. 4

new finance, transformed his company into the impressively-titled 'Società Torinese Automobili Rapid', took over the Bianchi Steelworks in 1904, and began producing 'Rapid' cars in their factory on the Barriera di Nizza in Turin. But Giovanni Battista was already in poor health, and consequently left STAR a year later to retire to Bordighera, where he died in 1912.

Young Giacinto Ghia joined STAR as a tester, a job demanding some degree of technical skill, for STAR was a well-founded company technically—it was headed by the engineers Giovanni Battista Maggi and Rodolfo Chio—and its products, handsome round-radiatored cars with some sporting pretensions, were well-built and highly-regarded. It had proved, however, an unlucky STAR for Chio, killed during 1906 in a stupid accident while testing a new car.

At STAR, Giacinto Ghia was able to indulge his passion for cars; there was even the opportunity for some motor sport. One of the few extant photographs of this enigmatic _carrozziere_ shows him at the wheel of a stripped 2.6 litre Rapid 15 hp at a 1911 Modena speed event.

Shortly before the outbreak of World War I, Ghia left the Barriera di Nizza to join Diatto, offshoot of an 80-year-old firm of coachbuilders and tram-makers which had begun building cars, under the name 'Torino' in 1905 under licence from Adolphe Clément of France. Before long, the company was putting its own name on its cars, and Clément finally severed his connection with Diatto in 1909.

Ghia's spell with Diatto ended abruptly in 1915, for he overturned the car he was testing and broke both his legs in the crash: seriously injured and unable to drive, he was out of a job. Fate, however, now dealt more kindly with him, for the Diatto company was expanding rapidly and, in a series of moves which included the acquisition of the John Newton company (formerly Valt) of Turin and Scacchi of Chivasso, it opened a new coach-building activity in the via Moretta. Moreover, despite the war, Diatto managed to continue the production of motor vehicles, building military trucks; Rapid, on the other hand, concentrated on the manufacture of shells, though it was noted that the company's entire truck production had been acquired by that well-known Alsatian entrepreneur and erstwhile collaborator of Ettore Bugatti, Emile Mathis of Strasbourg (since Alsace was at that time under German control, it's difficult to know which side of the hostilities those Rapid trucks ended up on. . .).

Giacinto put his early training as a coachbuilder to good use, subcontracting to build the _scocca_—the wooden framework—of car bodies for Diatto. He rented a little workshop on the via Pettiti, where he managed to survive through the difficult years of the Great War, planning for an expansion of the business once peace came. Still barely 30 in 1918, Ghia had already gained a reputation as 'an exceptional seeker of the new and beautiful, particularly attracted towards the production of luxury cars'.

About this time, Ghia gained a partner, a shadowy figure named Gariglio about whom nothing is known except that the name is apparently common among Torinese butchers (and since the first backer of what ultimately became AC cars in Britain was a butcher from Norwood named Portwine, maybe Signor Gariglio's part in the venture was merely the prosaic—but essential—one of provider of finance). Certainly Ghia & Gariglio expanded rapidly, moving in 1921 to new premises at 4 Corso Valentino (since renamed

ABOVE An early contract for Ghia & Gariglio was for the production of landaulette bodies for the SPA Tipo 23, a 2724 cc sidevalve four current between 1920–25

BELOW This pretty flared-wing _Gran Sport_ four-seater was built by Ghia & Gariglio on the 4951 cc Lancia Kappa chassis in 1922

13

Spider-Cabriolet a due posti
per
S. A. R. il Duca di Pistoia
su châssis FIAT "520„

GHIA

CARROZZERIA DI LUSSO

CORSO VALENTINO 5-6 - TORINO

This somewhat pedestrian two-seater 'Spider-Cabriolet' was built for his Highness the Duke of Pistoia on a 2244 cc Fiat 520 chassis in 1928.

Corso Marconi, and now the site of Fiat's headquarters).

Moreover, the little coachbuilding business which 'quickly established a clientele of refined lovers of sporting coachwork', saw its first success in 1921 with a contract to build the bodies for Fiat's new sporting derivative of their mass-produced 501 model, the 501S, whose side valve engine developed, thanks to a high-compression head, a dizzy 26 bhp (compared with 23 bhp for the standard Tipo 501). Rather like its French contemporary the Citroën Caddy, the 501S was a boat-tailed torpedo whose sporting properties lay more in its appearance than in its performance; a top speed of 57 mph was claimed in standard form. Careful tuning repaid dividends, however, since by fitting a Silvani ohv conversion, the car could be persuaded to top 89 mph, and a 501S was the first competition car of that great Czech driver Madame Elisabeth Junek (though she threw most of Ghia's pretty bodywork away to save weight!) Apart from the 'regular' 501S, Ghia & Gariglio also pro-

This sports saloon by Carrozzeria
Ghia was fitted to the new 2.5 litre
Fiat 521 chassis in 1928

duced a racing derivative of the 501S, with wire wheels and a vast external exhaust pipe.

Nor was the Fiat 501S the only 'series' production undertaken by Ghia and Gariglio, for in February 1922 the little company advertised the fact that it was building the series-produced landaulette bodywork for the SPA Tipo 23.

Later that year, Ghia & Gariglio turned out a flared-wing 'Gran Sport' body on a Lancia Kappa chassis, commenting: 'Even on sporting models, today's clientele demands comfort and refinement; here is a model which combines these qualities with fine sober and modern lines, built by Carrozzeria Ghia & Gariglio of Turin.' Such 'non-mass-produced elegant and rational coachwork on the latest design of cars', established Ghia's reputation for creative style; the claim that the company was experienced in building '*gran sport*' bodywork was borne out by Giacinto Ghia's involvement in motor sport.

Having come across an illustration of Giacinto Ghia showing him, face concealed by a racing mask, competing in the Targa Florio at the wheel of a Diatto, I wrote to Nino Vaccarella, the local hero of the Targa—whom I'd met in Sicily in 1983—in his present day capacity as vice president of the Automobile Club Palermo and asked whether he could shed some light on Ghia's Targa participation. By return came a sheaf of photostats detailing Ghia's exploits in the Sicilian classic. He had competed in two Targas—1919 and 1921—both times driving Diattos. Almost certainly, he had also built their racing bodywork.

Even though during 1919 Diatto had built a number of Type 13 Bugattis under licence—the 'luxurious roomy' saloon model shown in that year's Paris Salon carried bodywork that bore the hallmarks of Ghia's contemporary design—it wasn't one of these lively voiturettes that Giacinto Ghia drove in the 1919 Targa, but a 25 hp Diatto Tipo 4DC, a somewhat ponderous device with a 2724 cc side-valve power unit, and 'tuned', it seems, merely by the substitution of sketchy racing bodywork for the standard item.

L'ALFA-ROMEO " 6 C-1500 ,, del Sig. F. Pirola di Mi-
lano, con carrozzeria leggerissima tutta in alluminio recante
le ruote di scorta racchiuse nella parte posteriore, che
conquistò il PRIMO POSTO - classe 1500 cmc. - nella

COPPA DELLE MILLE MIGLIA 1929

GHIA ~ CARROZZERIA DI LUSSO ~ CORSO VALENTINO, 4 ~ TORINO

RIGHT Class winner in the 1929
Mille Miglia was this elegant 6C1500
Alfa Romeo which concealed its
spare wheel in its pointed tail

RIGHT Ghia was firmly established
as one of Italy's leading
coachbuilders by the end of the
1920s; the Ghia two-seater Lancia
Lambda Cabriolet (top) compares
well with the other concours winning
cars by Ghia's great rival of the day,
Farina, also pictured here

VETTURE PREMIATE AI RECENTI CONCORSI D'ELEGANZA

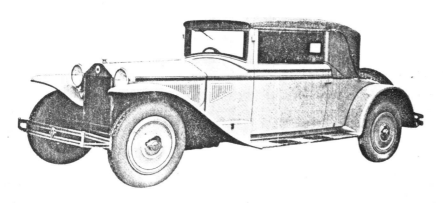

(dall'alto in basso) *Cabriolet* a due posti su LANCIA *"Lambda,,* del Dott. Arturo Rinaldi, costruito dalla Carrozzeria GHIA, tra i primi classificati nell'ultimo Concorso dell'A. C. di Roma — *Brougham* su *"Lambda,,* del Sen. Romeo Gallenga Stuart, fuori concorso, e *Cabriolet "All Weather,,* pure su *"Lambda,,* di Donna Myriam Potenziani, primo della III categoria del Concorso romano, entrambi costruiti da FARINA, — Guida interna sport FARINA, su ISOTTA FRASCHINI del Conte Felice Trossi; primo premio al recente Concorso Internaz. di Montecarlo

That 1919 Targa (held on 23 November because Cavaliere Vicenzo Florio was determined that his first postwar race should take place *that* year), was the very event in which André Boillot—younger brother of the bombastic Georges, 'the spirit of France in motor racing', shot down on the Western Front in 1916—crossed the finishing line at high speed backwards in his Peugeot, having rammed the corner of the grandstand and injured 'two guardian soldiers and other spectators' who had crowded on to the track. He was sent back to cross the line in the conventional direction before he was declared the winner.

It also saw the appearance of a young racing driver called Enzo Ferrari, who started first and finished eighth at the wheel of a CMN.

Giacinto Ghia, however, missed his chance for sporting glory that day, for his Diatto failed to complete the first lap of the Medio Madonie course, though his team-mate Gamboni managed to finish third overall, as well as winning his class, in an identical car (not bad, considering it was the marque's debut in international racing).

Commented the sporting magazine *Motori Aeri Cicli & Sport*: 'The very brave Sig. Ghia hadn't a chance to let his qualities shine through, for he was the victim of an incident at the end of the first lap. At Polizzi, in order to avoid an imprudent kid who ran across the street, Sig. Ghia nobly swerved his car despite the risk to himself and ended up by smashing into a wall. He was unable to continue.'

Ghia fared rather better in his second (and final) Targa in 1921. For one

ABOVE One of the best-known small Italian sports cars of the early 1930s was the Fiat 508S; this Ghia-bodied example dates from 1933

RIGHT ABOVE A more unusual body style for the Fiat 501S 'Ballila' chassis was this 'Mille Miglia' two-seater coupé built by Ghia in 1933

RIGHT The Itala 65 which won the Concours d'Elegance at Villa d'Este in 1929

6

27

Spider sport aerodinamico della **Carrozzeria Ghia** su **Lancia** " Augusta " (si veda pure a pag. 18) ● (a destra) Particolare d'una berlina aerodinamica pure di **Ghia** su " Augusta "

fatto sta che nel suo *spider* color giallino, costruito da Pinin su *châssis* " Astura ", la signora stava assai bene. Una bella macchina ed una guidatrice in carattere con essa rallegrano sempre il cuore dei tecnici. Questo *spider* aveva il paravento a punta ed i parafanghi a goccia. Era privo delle pedane.

■ Nelle carrozzerie degli *Stabilimenti Farina,* alcune delle quali veramente ammirevoli, abbiamo trovato forse il migliore trattamento dei parafanghi anteriori. Essi sono del tipo a parte anteriore rigonfia, cui abbiamo accennato più sopra. Ma non si tratta che d'un particolare. La vera caratteristica delle vetture dovute agli *Stabilimenti* non è facile a descrivere. Si tratta di un equilibrio dell'insieme, di un senso della misura, di uno studio tutto speciale della linea in vista di ottenere soluzioni classicamente moderne. La berlina su "Astura" presentata dal sig. M. Antolini Ossi era un magnifico esempio della produzione *Farina*. Essa aveva lo schermo di radiatore arrotondato, i fari profilati, e la coda uso *spider*. Colorazione in nero e grigio scuro. Altra riuscitissima vettura era un *cabriolet* a quattro posti, anch'esso a coda, nel quale il mantice si poteva aprire o chiudere automaticamente, grazie al dispositivo elettro-idraulico brevettato dagli *Stabilimenti* stessi. Ma su tale congegno torneremo presto, perchè merita un'accurata descrizione tecnica.

E veniamo alla più sorprendente creazione presentata al Concorso. Essa era una berlina veramente aerodinamica, costruita da *Viotti* su *Alfa-Romeo* modello " Pescara ". Ne diamo parecchie fotografie perchè il lettore possa farsi un'idea di questa macchina straordinaria. Il disegno di tale vettura fu una particolare fatica dell'ing. Rolandi, il Capo-pilota dell'*Aeronautica d'Italia*. Si tratta di un tentativo molto co-

raggioso e lodevole, il quale è costato parecchio ed ha insegnato diverse cose. Esteticamente, la macchina è piena di slancio e d'eleganza. A noi è parsa buona anche in fatto di profilatura. L'abitabilità è ottima, e il paravento

(sotto) Guida interna della **Carrozzeria Casaro** su **Lancia** " Augusta " ● Cabriolet a quattro posti degli **Stabilimenti Garavini** su **Fiat** "Balilla"

thing, the race was held at a more propitious time of year—29 May—and for another, he actually managed to complete the course. His mount this time was a far more sporting proposition than the ponderous machine he had driven in 1919, for it was a Diatto 4DS, whose power unit, though basically similar to that of the 4DA, was tuned to develop 50 bhp instead of 30, and could turn at 3000 rpm against 2000. That boosted its top speed to 140–150 km/h instead of 90; a horseshoe-shaped radiator shell gave the car quite a Bugatti look (though the only official collaboration between Diatto and Bugatti had been a vastly unsuccessful wartime aeroengine and the construction of those few Type 13 voiturettes under licence).

Ghia finished 16th, having covered the 482 km course in 9 hr 5 min 15 sec; he was, nevertheless, 1 hr 40 min behind the winner, Masetti's Fiat, and his fastest lap of the 108 km circuit, at 2 hr 8 min 54 sec, was precisely 1 sec slower than that of Fracassi's Model T Ford, and represented an average speed of some 31 mph!

By 1922, it seems, the partnership between Ghia and Gariglio was foundering, the company attempting to bolster its income by taking on the Italian agency for Meyrowitz racing goggles, 'as used by all the world champions in motoring, aviation, motorcycling and cycling'; among their clientele was the legendary Felice Nazzaro, who won the 1922 French Grand Prix in a 2-litre Fiat, and his motorcycling champion nephew Biagio Nazzaro, who was killed in a similar car in the same race when the back axle fractured.

Around 1923, Gariglio left the partnership, and Ghia was on his own;

ABOVE An elegant Cabriolet *Gran Lusso* constructed on a short-chassis Alfa Romeo 2300B by Carrozzeria Ghia in 1937

ABOVE LEFT This aerodynamic 'Spider Sport' (left) was built on the Lancia Augusta chassis by Ghia in 1935, while the detail (right) shows the faired-in headlamps used on a streamlined Ghia Augusta saloon. The other two cars are from other stables and show less development in their styling: (top) Lancia by Casaro and (bottom) Fiat by Garavini

The ultimate in late-30s chic—a
Ghia cabriolet on the newly-
introduced Lancia Aprilia; such
open bodies tended to age badly on
the Aprilia chassis, since they lacked
the rigidity of the integral-
construction Aprilia saloon

at that time his little factory employed some 30 people turning out two to
three bodies a month. His principal assistant was a man named Giorgio
Alberti who was to stay with Ghia for two decades.

During the latter part of the 1920s, Ghia established both a considerable
reputation and a titled clientele; early in 1928 the company produced a neat
two-seater Spider-Cabriolet for HRH the Duke of Pistoia on the new six-
cylinder Fiat 520 chassis; a limited series of 'berlines de luxe' was constructed
on the improved Tipo 521 chassis between 1928 and 1931.

In 1929 _Motor Italia_ described Ghia as 'one of those Torinese coachbuilders whose work bears the imprint of great distinction'. That was in
relation to a portent of things to come exhibited at the Rome Salon, 'a superb
coupé de ville which can practically be converted into a saloon car, built
on the new Chrysler 75 chassis'. The Chrysler marque was to be of great
significance in Ghia's future.

The same year, Ghia won a prize at the Automobile Club of Rome's concours with an elegant two-seater cabriolet on a Lancia Lambda belonging
to Dr Arturo Rinaldi; another trophy gained that season was at the Concorso
di Villa d'Este where a coupé spyder on an Itala 65 chassis won its class
and a gold shield.

Nor did Ghia lack sporting success, for in the 1929 Mille Miglia an Alfa
Romeo 6C1500 belonging to F. Pirola of Milan, with 'superlight coachwork

A traditional Ghia design, this pillarless sports on the Alfa 6C2500 is said by its makers to have been built in 1939–40; the faired-in headlamps seem to indicate a date later in the Alfa's 1939–53 production life

entirely made of aluminium with the spare wheels housed in the rear of the bodywork' won the 1500 cc class: its flared wings and pointed tail evoked distinct echoes of the old 501S Fiat.

The end of the year 1929 saw the construction of a handsome transformable torpedo on an Isotta Fraschini 8A chassis to the order of HRH the Duke of Bergamo; this had its two spare wheels mounted out back behind the luggage boot, which certainly gave the car a degree of flamboyance, but also showed a cavalier disregard for any problems associated with excessive rear overhang. At the same time, Ghia produced a particularly attractive Spider Tipo Corsa on the 6C 1750 Alfa chassis. Its sharply raked windscreen was a neat and advanced touch.

By now Ghia coachwork was recognized as being in the front rank of design. In February 1930, *Motor Italia* devoted a double page spread to Ghia designs under the heading, 'If you want not just a good, safe automobile but a beautiful car, consult a true artist'. . . .

The article began: 'We have to confess a weakness for beautiful coachwork. The automobile itself is not enough; we want the beautiful car, created by an artist passionately in love with the marvellous machines that characterize the age in which we live . . . just as a beautiful woman badly dressed loses some of her fascination, so a quality chassis, badly bodied, attracts less. As the great couturiers have to study closely which clothes and which colours

best suit different types of woman, so the artistic _carrozziere_ must interpret
every model of chassis in a different manner. Only then will the finished
car conserve and enhance the fundamental characteristics—that is to say,
the personality—of the model. . . . An ordinary coachbuilder can make an
accurate and diligent job with all the toil and patience of a worthy artisan,
but just compare the same chassis clothed by a great _carrozziere_ . . . the recent
and most successful creations of Carrozzeria Ghia of Turin illustrated on
these pages readily show the class of our most distinguished coachbuilders.
Compare these spiders, these cabriolets, these saloons with other, less aristo-
cratic models that we see daily on our streets, and you'll notice that not
all coachbuilders possess the intuition, the good taste and the sense of
equilibrium of a master like Ghia. The Spider Sport on an Alfa-Romeo chassis is a jewel indeed; its lines epitomize youth and speed.'

But Ghia was about to gain a rival: in 1931, young Pinin Farina broke
away from the old-established family firm, Stabilimenti Farina, and set up
on his own account. Like Ghia, Pinin Farina followed the modern line in
coachbuilding, with such features as steeply raked windscreens; working for
him was a young designer, Felice Mario Boano, who after only a year moved
on to establish his own woodworking shop, in which he made body frames
not only for Pinin Farina but also for Ghia, with whom he became close
friends.

'Ghia,' recalled Boano, 'was a good friend and a great worker, but not
much of an administrator—I had to help him sometimes. . . .'

At the Turin concours of 1933, Ghia created another sensation with his
class-winning two-seater 'Mille Miglia' sports coupé on the brand new Tipo

Another difficult-to-date Ghia
design, this rather ugly Alfa Romeo
6C2500 Sport Spyder probably dates
from just after the war, though its
makers claim a date of 1939–40 for it

508 Fiat 'Balilla' chassis; its steeply-raked windscreen contrasted dramatically with the vertical line of the rear of the passenger compartment.

During the late 1930s, Ghia hit its peak production, the little factory turning out 8–10 cars a month; 1935 saw a particularly neat 'spider sport aerodinamico' on the Lancia Augusta, with pontoon wings and a finned boot lid that recalled Ghia's famous two-seater sports body on the 508S Balilla chassis. There was also an aerodynamic berline on the Augusta chassis, with faired-in lamps and horizontal bonnet louvres.

The theme was carried on into the new Aprilia, which in standard unitary-construction saloon guise had a notably short bonnet over its narrow V4 power unit; Ghia remedied this impediment to truly exotic proportions on the two-seat cabriolet shown at the 1937 Milan Salone dell'Automobile by carrying the crocodile bonnet back over the scuttle to the base of the fold-flat windscreen, while giving a feeling of length by adopting an impressive rear overhang.

The same year Ghia adopted similar lines for a cabriolet 'Gran Lusso' on the 2300B Alfa Romeo; in 1938 a somewhat plebeian four-seat convertible coupé was built on the six-cylinder 2.8 litre Fiat chassis which treated rearward vision with cavalier disdain—its back window bore a strong resemblance to a glazed letter-box!

Immediately before the outbreak of war, Ghia produced a beautifully-proportioned pillarless sports saloon on the 2.5 litre Alfa Romeo chassis, but manufacture of luxury cars was one of the first casualties of the hostilities. Giacinto Ghia managed to avoid getting seriously embroiled in the Fascist war machine, and his unglamorous wartime production consisted of the

In similar vein to the car opposite, this Alfa-Romeo 6C2500 cabriolet is again said to date from 1939–40; it's difficult to guess the rationale behind the odd air intake designs on these two cars

manufacture of carts for the Italian army. There was, however, a profitable, if highly unofficial, sideline in the building of bicycles for the black market. . . .

With its concentration of car factories, Turin was a natural target for long-range bombing raids by the Allies, and the little plant in the Corso Valentino was hit seven times; in 1943, a bomber scored a direct hit on the Ghia works, 'and all that was left of 25 years' work was smoking ruins'.

Giacinto Ghia was naturally deeply affected by the loss: evacuated to the outskirts of Turin, he had just returned to supervise the rebuilding of his factory when he was suddenly taken ill and died on 21 February, 1944. Ghia was only 56: 'all who knew him will remember his open character and firm strength of will,' commented an obituary.

There had been, however, a hidden side to the exemplary Signor Ghia's existence: many years later, when Ford design staff were working at the Ghia plant, recalls Dearborn design man Tom Land, they used to frequent a little night-club in central Turin. The old lady who ran the club noticed the little enamel Ghia badges they wore in their lapels: 'You are from Carrozzeria Ghia?' she asked. When the Ford men told her that they were indeed working at Ghia, the old lady brightened: 'You see, I was Giacinto Ghia's mistress!'

Yet another Ghia interpretation of the Alfa Romeo 6C2500, this 'Sport Berlina' is definitely postwar, and foreshadows the Ghia Plymouth XX-500 that brought Ghia and Chrysler together

2 Up from the ashes

With the plant destroyed and her husband dead, Ghia's widow took rapid steps to safeguard the one thing that was left intact: the good name of the company. She offered the remnants of the firm to Ghia's good friends Giorgio Alberti and Felice Mario Boano; Boano immediately left his woodworking company to get on with its business and moved to Ghia. Since nothing remained, Boano took the eminently sensible decision that to rebuild the factory on the original site would take too long and leave the company at a considerable disadvantage when it came to making the most of the inevitable postwar demand for new motorcars. So he transferred operations under the name 'Carrozzeria Succ. Ghia' to a new site on the via Tommaso Grossi, and declared his aim of keeping to Ghia's original philosophy of producing cars in limited numbers but of high quality. By the beginning of 1946, commented *Motor Italia*, the revived company was 'ready to resume its battle station in that peaceful contest where the habitability and good sense of Torinese coachwork will quickly be triumphant once again'.

The new location had the great advantage of being close to the railway, so that bodies could readily be shipped abroad, for the company was beginning to look at export markets for the first time, and tentative links were being forged with French manufacturers.

Boano was quick off the mark with new bodies which perfectly captured the postwar mood for a touch of flamboyance to compensate for all the privations of wartime; his particular hallmark was the enclosure of all four wheels behind metal 'blister' fairings which could be hinged up out of the way when changing a wheel. Opulently 'soft' in line, both open and closed bodies were built in this style on a variety of chassis. In some cases, 'overbodied' was almost too mild a term to use, for Boano's bodywork virtually swamped the chassis that bore it, like the Fiat 1500 2/4 seat drophead (the rear two seats hidden beneath a metal fairing) that made a sensational appearance at the Lausanne '*Jour d'Elegance*' in 1946.

The following year, a sister car, 'a superb cabriolet painted scarlet lake', competed with honour in a concours in Turin's Giardino Reale.

Even more extreme was the cabriolet built round this time on an Alfa Romeo 6C 2500 SS chassis; a limited series of these low and wide two-seaters was constructed between 1946 and 1950. The blisters over the front wheels continued on into a swaged moulding blending into the rear wheel arch and

LEFT Ghia's postwar recovery under
Felice Mario Boana was little short
of miraculous—by 1946 the
company was turning out
flamboyant designs like this Fiat
1500 sport saloon

LEFT BELOW This delightful Lancia
Aprilia Coupé Sport was built by
Ghia right at the end of the model's
production life in 1950

BELOW Another example of Boano's
use of faired-in wheels is this Talbot
Lago Record saloon of the early
1950s

FOTO MONCALVO TORINO

LEFT Built in 1946–47, this 4/5 seater cabriolet is based on the Fiat 1500 chassis, despite the Alfa-like grille

ABOVE A more confident interpretation designed by Boano on the Fiat 1500 chassis, this 1946 Cabriolet Gran Sports conceals two extra seats beneath the metal cover behind the cockpit

LEFT Boano's blister fairings swung well out of the way when access to the wheels was required, as this 1947 Alfa 6C2500 Cabriolet demonstrates

ABOVE Elegant side view of a
Delahaye 235, one of the few car
chassis built by this French
manufacturer in 1951–52, clad in
pillarless 4/5 seat Ghia saloon
coachwork

LEFT The styling is similar but the
chassis is different: this pillarless
saloon is based on one of the last
Lancia Aprilias, built in 1950

BELOW A new trend for the 1950s:
this 4/5 seat Supergioello fastback
saloon is built on the Fiat 1400
chassis

a decorative chrome moulding accentuated the length of the car.

And the 1947 Coupé Royale built by Succ. Ghia was commended by *Motor Italia* for its 'rationally profiled lines, large windows and light, entirely metal, construction'.

Perhaps the last of these exaggerated cabriolet bodies was built on a 235 Delahaye (which in itself was one of the last private cars from this renowned French maker) in 1951–52.

Boano also designed a number of pillarless coupés in the same idiom on the Lancia Aprilia and Fiat 1500; and maintained his connection with French luxury car manufacturers by building a pillarless Berline on a Lago Record, though this had rather a high roof line, which spoilt the flowing elegance of the basic design.

These cars were very definitely designed for the world of the concours d'elegance, but Boano was equally capable of designing purposeful sports cars. Particularly successful in appearance was a delightful sports car on a late Lancia Aprilia chassis whose lines look modern even today (though the spartan dashboard layout with its oversized dials and minimal controls and the prominent chrome hubcaps have aged less happily).

A little later came a sport coupé on the same chassis; where the open car had used a stylized Lancia grille, the closed version had a wide oval grille which made the car look quite different, even though the general lines of the body were very similar. The two cars were dramatic proof of Boano's skill in designing bodywork for totally disparate types of motoring.

Ghia could work in more formal idioms, too, a fact underlined in 1950 by a commission to build an official limousine for the President of Italy on one of the first Lancia Aurelia chassis to be produced; even though the Aurelia had a 1991 cc power unit against the 1486 cc of the later Aprilias, it must have been hard-pushed to stir this ponderous state car about its business.

The close collaboration between Boano and Fiat bore particularly happy results in a series of sporting cabriolets called the Gioiello and Supergioiello which were the forerunners of what has become regarded as the typical Italian line of the 1950s; it appears that the Gioiello was based on the Fiat 1100, while the slightly more square cut Supergioiello was built on the Fiat 1400 chassis.

But Ghia's work with Italian manufacturers was not restricted to Fiat, for in 1950 the company built its first Ferrari body, a classically elegant two-door Berlinetta 195 Inter which foreshadowed the flowing lines which were adopted by other makers of high performance sports cars during the 1950s: Stabilimenti Farina, for instance, built a similar two-seater coupé on a Jowett Jupiter chassis shown at the 1951 Paris Salon, and described as 'most sporting'.

In the next two or three years, says Ghia design engineer Manfred Lampe, Ghia built at least 25 Ferrari Berlinettas, eleven of them on the 195 Inter chassis, eight on the 212 Inter and five on the 340 America, for which the basic design had to be stretched, losing some of its lithe elegance in the process.

Two Ferrari cabriolets were derived from the Berlinetta, one of them shown at Turin in 1952; the overall effect was somewhat spoilt by excessively fussy grille design.

LEFT ABOVE One of the prettiest of all the 25 or so Ghia-bodied Ferraris is this two-door Berlinetta on the 195 Inter chassis dating from 1950

LEFT BELOW Torinese oddity: Ghia saloon bodywork on the rear-engined Lancia A-10 prototype of 1950 can hardly be said to be elegant in appearance

Nor were the Berlinas that Ghia built on the 212 Inter and 340 America a great success: only four (possibly six) were made. Additionally, a two-door, four-seater saloon on the Type 342, the long wheelbase version of the America, appeared at the Paris Salon in 1951. It was, said *The Autocar*, 'finished in light and dark blue in a manner which emphasizes the fineness of line'. The engine was the low compression version of the 4.1 litre Ferrari V12, developing 'a mere 180 bhp instead of the customary 220, but should have no difficulty propelling a four-seater saloon by Ghia, weighing slightly under a ton, at speeds which will be difficult of attainment by any other four-seater saloon in the world'.

And a photograph in the Ghia archives reveals a facet of their prototype work for local manufacturers in the shape of a two-door Berlinetta on Lancia's experimental rear-engined A-10 chassis, which never went into production. The awkward proportions revealed in the picture perhaps explain why the model was stillborn; pull-out ventilating louvres ahead of the rear wheelarches suggest possible overheating problems.

Despite the connections with France, Ghia still remained basically a bodybuilder for the Torinese trade; but the events of 1950 would change all that. Attempting to recover from the damage of wartime, Fiat had asked Chrysler in America for assistance in the training of its technicians in the latest machining and assembly techniques. In return, Chrysler decided that it lacked the styling and bodybuilding expertise that was found in Turin, and established contacts with Pinin Farina and Ghia.

To handle the newly-forged links with Chrysler, Boano brought in Luigi Segre, a remarkable designer/businessman aged only 30. Commercial director of the SIATA tuning company and *pilota gentleman*, Segre had been liaison officer with an American army group operating with the Italian resistance during the war. A far-sighted entrepreneur, Segre felt that the future of the company should be based on a far wider clientele than the European market could offer. Consequently he took a ticket to America to build up his business relationships and became a close friend of Chrysler vice president C. B. Thomas, who handled the corporation's export sales.

In 1950, Segre and Boano designed a body on a Plymouth chassis which had been sent to Turin by Chrysler. As a demonstration of what Ghia could do in the way of one-off coachwork, the resultant four-door, six-light saloon, subsequently christened the XX-500, was hardly elegant—an Italian magazine described it as *pesante*. That useful portmanteau word of criticism translates variously, according to my dictionary, as 'heavy, weighty, lumpish, massive, ponderous, boring, wearisome', all of which aptly covered the XX-500, which was, it seems, based on a somewhat tedious series of special bodies designed by Ghia for the Fiat 1400 chassis.

But while Segre was keen to take on such foreign contracts to widen the influence of Ghia, Boano believed it should nurture its Torinese roots.

It's not difficult to see that there must have been personality differences between the two men, for Segre was quick-tempered and mercurial, and as impatient as any ambitious man whose poor health intimates that his time on earth may be limited. 'Segre coughed a lot,' recalls Ghia's present head, Filippo Sapino, who joined the company as a designer in 1960. 'But when he was angry he would shout so loud that he could be heard all over the plant—the walls would literally tremble!'

RIGHT This three-seater Fiat 1400 cabriolet was one of a short series built by Ghia in 1951, all differing slightly in the decorative treatment of the side panels

BELOW This ponderous-looking saloon is the Plymouth XX-500 designed by Segre and Boano which sparked off Ghia's long relationship with the Chrysler Corporation. Note the curious radiator mascot, which appears to be a stylised sailing ship

LEFT Obviously inspired by Ghia's concept car work for Chrysler, this streamlined Fiat 1100 Abarth sport coupé was exhibited on the Ghia stand at the 1953 Turin show

LEFT ABOVE This purposeful little two-seater Gioello sports coupé was built on the Fiat 1100 chassis in 1948

LEFT BELOW The Ghia Supergioello models of the late 1940s were based on the Fiat 1500 chassis

LEFT AND BELOW Two views of the
preliminary clay model for the
Chrysler K-310 photographed in
Virgil Exner's studio in Detroit in
1952

It had been Boano who had developed the fastback body for the Lancia Aurelia B20 coupé, first shown in prototype form in 1951, and, according to a contemporary Ghia leaflet, 'put into production with few modifications'. That's true: but large-scale production didn't emanate from Ghia, for the little plant on the via Tommaso Grossi just couldn't cope with building cars in large numbers. The order for the first 100 B20 Lancia coupés only was given to Ghia, who actually built bodyshells for 98 of them, which were finished and trimmed by Carrozzeria Viotti; as Ghia was seeking to remain a free-wheeling centre for the design and development of prototypes, manufacture in bulk of the B20 was turned over to Pinin Farina, which had become an 'industrialized' coachbuilder (and the cars, in any case, did not carry the insignia of any _carrozzeria_).

Another Boano project that would subsequently bear rich fruit for others was a prototype sports coupé on the Alfa Romeo Giulietta, shown at the 1952 Turin Salon. That design formed the basis for the Giulietta Sprint offered as a prize to 200 lucky debenture holders from among those whose cash was being used to finance Alfa's new mass-produced Berlina. The order for production of the lottery cars went to Nuccio Bertone, since Ghia couldn't handle even the intended run of 500 Giuliettas. But the car proved so popular that the 500 eventually grew into a total of 40,000 Giulietta Sprints, built between 1954 and 1965. That order put Bertone into the big time as an 'industrialized coachbuilder'. Ghia, who had created the original design but was incapable of exploiting it, remained as a small _carrozzeria_. . . .

Early in 1953 Boano decided to withdraw from Ghia in order to devote

Not the prettiest body ever fitted to the Silver Wraith Rolls-Royce, perhaps, but the inscription on the back of this 1953 photograph states that this Ghia limousine was built for King Farouk of Egypt

RIGHT Gigi Segre (leaning on the truck tailboard) seems vastly happy that the 1952 Chrysler C-200 convertible is being shipped to America: he's mercifully unaware that the American dockers will accidentally drop it on the quayside when it's unloaded in New York . . .

LEFT This view of the clay for one concept for the Chrysler K-310 shows Exner's favoured spare wheel mounting in the boot lid

LEFT Another K-310 proposal showing a different front-end treatment closer to the finished car

himself more closely to Fiat, and consequently split ownership of the company between three partners: his son Paolo and Segre took 40 per cent each, while a Ghia executive named Sibilla had the remaining 20 per cent.

Again, there were personality clashes; Segre and Sibilla couldn't get along together, and it was quickly decided that Segre should be allowed to buy up the shares held by his partners in instalments; by the end of 1953 he was in complete control, with financial backing from the owner of the Monviso metal stamping plant, Casalis.

But the disagreements between Ghia's executives were obviously kept concealed behind the scenes, for Chrysler president Kaufmann T. Keller had been sufficiently impressed by the Ghia craftsmanship and modest cost — about $10,000 — incorporated in that _pesante_ XX-500 to permit stylist Virgil

M. Exner, who had been brought in by Keller to revive Chrysler's design image, to proceed with the commissioning of other Chrysler-based concept cars from the Torinese carrozzeria. Exner set up an advanced styling group which also included Cliff Voss and Maury Baldwin: associated with them was the intuitive engineer Paul Farago, who ran a 'specialty sports car shop' not far from Detroit and, more importantly, could speak Italian and thus interpreted for Exner in his dealings with Segre and Boano.

While searching in the dusty archive room which adjoins what used to be Segre's offices in the Ghia plant, I came across a pile of 35-year-old photographs tossed in the bottom of a stationery cupboard. They were the original Chrysler prints of the three-eighths scale clay models created in Highland Park, Detroit, and shipped over to Turin for Ghia to translate into metal.

ABOVE First of all the Chrysler-Ghia dream cars, the K-310 of 1952, based on the new hemi-head V8 Saratoga chassis and aimed at reviving Chrysler's flagging design image

LEFT Ghia built two Chrysler SS ('Styling Specials') in 1952 at the request of C. B. Thomas, Chrysler's director of export sales; the model starred at that year's Paris Salon

LEFT BELOW Another Exner design, the Plymouth Explorer appeared in 1952: its grille was supposed to suggest the nose of a shark

BELOW The four-seated Dodge 'Red Ram' Firebomb convertible of 1953 was the fore-runner of the limited production Dual-Ghia model

They gave the lie to the cast legend 'Chrysler model—created by Ghia' attached to the bodywork of the first Chryslers bodied in Turin in 1952. Exner had designed the bodies in their entirety: these old photographs made it quite clear that Chrysler had simply bought Ghia's expertise in forming metal, and that the Turin design input into these early Ghia-built Chrysler bodies was absolutely nil.

Nevertheless, those Torinese panel-beating skills were well worth exploiting, for they are the product of centuries of experience, going back to the armourers of the Middle Ages who could form steel breastplates over a log and who had been the direct ancestors of the Piedmont region's rural metal-workers, the *calderai*, who still produce vases, bowls and kitchen utensils from beaten brass and copper.

For the *carrozziere*, those skills translate into the ability to execute complex metal panels over simple wooden formers with marvellous dexterity to the extent that compound curvatures can be turned out that are perfect enough to have been pressed out rather than hammered. . . .

That first Exner design, the K-310, appeared in 1952; the 'K' in its name was a tribute to Kaufman T. Keller, the recently-retired president of Chrysler, the '310' a hopeful reference to the engine's putative power output (in fact, it only developed some 180 bhp). A sleekly attractive sports coupé, the K-310 was based on the new hemi-head V8 Saratoga chassis, and cost $20,000 to build at Ghia; its styling was, I feel, inspired by the 'Superleggera Aerlux' coupé on an Isotta Fraschini Monterosa chassis exhibited at the 1947 Paris Saloon by Touring of Milan.

Some of the design features of the K-310 like the egg-crate grille and 'gun-sight' prismatic rear lamps would eventually find their way into production, but its basic purpose was more fundamental than mere kite-flying for future models. As a functional, practical 'dream car', it was intended to demonstrate to the show-going public that Chrysler really cared about contemporary design, because there was sound evidence that Chrysler's dowdy

Exner's favourite project—the 2 + 2 Ghia DeSoto Adventurer I of 1952, which failed to make production because it wasn't vulgar enough. So Virgil Exner retained it as his personal car for three years

design image was costing it sales in the States, despite the company's sound record of advanced engineering.

Another feature of the K-310 that would appear on future production Chryslers was the spare-wheel housing in the boot-lid. At least, the shape of the spare wheel was formed in the lid on production cars; the wheel itself was moved to the floor of the boot at an early stage of the development programme.

The rare and handsome convertible version of the K-310, the C-200, merely had a spare wheel shape embossed in the boot lid as a styling feature. Painted pale green and black, the C-200 was shipped to New York aboard the _SS Constitution_—and was accidentally dropped on the quayside as it was being unloaded, but survived to star in exhibitions in Chrysler dealerships around America.

Nevertheless, the first K-310 had the wheel-well in the boot lid, as did the contemporary 'Coupé d'Elegance' Chrysler, a vehicle of stupendous impracticality in which the obvious disadvantages of mounting the spare wheel in the boot lid were eliminated by doing away with the boot lid itself and carrying the wheel on an ingenious linkage. When the lid over the wheel was opened, this heavyweight linkage was actuated by an hydraulic ram which occupied most of what would otherwise have been luggage space, to swing the wheel out over the rear bumper!

Exner's Ghia-Chryslers were pointing the way towards the 'letter car' muscle machinery of the mid-1950s, and this was particularly true of the Chrysler SS (or 'Styling Special') shown at the 1952 Paris Salon. Developed at the request of Segre's friend C. B. Thomas, the fastback SS was built on a cut-and-shut New Yorker chassis and its neat styling, with an 'open-mouthed' grille and a minimum of chrome was in direct contrast to the befinned 'dollar-grin' vulgarity that was typical of American car design at the period.

Chrysler went so far as to order a special run of 40 Ghia-Chryslers: but

Though it looked so quintessentially American, the DeSoto Adventurer II of 1954 was entirely designed at Ghia. And though it was so much longer than its predecessor, Adventurer II was only a two-seater

the commission was cut back because of the Korean War.

There were Ghia concept cars based on other Chrysler group chassis, too: Exner's two-seater Plymouth Explorer coupé appeared in 1952. *Torino Motori* commented: 'The front grille creates a first version of the "shark" look, whilst an attempt at lateral ornamentation runs down the whole of the sides.' The space where the rear seats would normally have been was occupied by two fitted suitcases, with roll-top storage boxes above the wheelarches.

Similar in overall appearance was Exner's first Dodge Firearrow roadster, which was built in 1953, and initially shown as a full-size mock-up. The original Firearrow, painted bright red, had a metallic grey moulding encircling the body with the two ends meeting at a bullet-shaped ornament in the centre of the front air intake. Equipped with twin headlamps below the moulding either side, it had tan leather upholstery; the second in the series had only single lamps. It was painted pale yellow with a black moulding, and had black leather upholstery; separate boots were provided for luggage and spare wheel, the luggage being stored behind the seats.

The two Firearrow roadsters were followed by a sport coupé, which reverted to quadruple headlamps, but gained a concave grille; its bumpers were no more than wide over-riders which, because they were actually set behind the thrust-forward grille, would have been of questionable value in a collision. This was perhaps more of a likelihood with this car than with many concept vehicles, since the Firearrow coupé was timed at a speed of 143 mph at the Chrysler proving grounds! The Firearrow series ended with a convertible, based on the coupé, but with jazzy black-and-white chequerboard upholstery.

Then there was the four-seat convertible Dodge 'Firebomb', of which a couple of versions were constructed during 1953, one of them with the aggressively-titled 'Red Ram' V8 engine, which were forerunners of the later 'Dual-Ghia' line.

Exner's favourite of all these early projects between Ghia and Chrysler was the DeSoto Adventurer I of 1952. This, said *Torino Motori*, 'was a sport coupé of very simple lines, and devoid of any decoration or ornamental mouldings, save for the chromed elements constituting the external exhaust pipes on either side.' Had this elegant design, a logical development of the K-310, gone forward for production, it would have been America's first 2 + 2 coupé: but its good taste, absence of vulgar ornamentation and minimal overhang front and rear were features diametrically opposed to what the average American car buyer wanted in the early 1950s, and so the Adventurer remained a prototype. Exner, however, was so taken with it that he used the Adventurer I as his personal car for three years. Don Kopka, now Ford vice president Design, worked with Exner in the 1950s and recalls taking the Adventurer to a concours at the Lime Rock race circuit, where the car was so different from anything else competing that a special class had to be created for it. Which it naturally won. . . .

Summing up this first phase of Ghia-Chrysler cooperation, *Torino Motori* commented: 'The Ghia line of these cars brought a note of gracefulness (*snellezza*, a marvellously evocative Italian word) to these elephantine American chassis, softening the intersections between the various elements of the car—wings, body, cockpit—and reducing the mass of chromed components

LEFT ABOVE This pretty Mille Miglia sports two-seater Lancia Aprilia was one of three built in 1947. One survives in England, another in Australia. Nardi e Danese made the tubular chassis

LEFT BELOW First shown as a full-scale mock-up with twin headlamps, the Dodge Firearrow II roadster was another of the one-offs that led to the Dual-Ghia

Commissioned by the King of
Saudia Arabia, this extended 1953
Cadillac Eldorado parade car lived
up to its name, with gold-plated
brightwork. Four door bodywork
was unusual, too

49

which characterize American cars of all periods (and which are of questionable aesthetic value) to rational proportions.'

As a footnote to this statement, which proved how well an American like Exner had captured the Italian skills of body design, a couple of years later, Ghia created an Adventurer II; this time, the car *was* designed in Turin, but had all the contemporary American kitsch details like ample overhangs and vulgar chrome rear lights like jet engine tailpipes. It also had the curious feature of a tinted plastic rear window that retracted electrically into the boot space! Ghia also paid Exner a sincere sideways tribute when they built a Ferrari coupé sport for the 1952 Paris Salon, for the lines of its two-tone body were very obviously derived from his Chrysler Special coupé!

But Ghia's links with foreign manufacturers weren't restricted to the Chrysler Corporation: during 1953, 'a year rich in satisfaction', Ghia also produced two special bodies for the Rolls-Royce Silver Wraith, 'moderating the angulosity and lightening the body pillars while conserving its distinctive and traditional characteristics' and built a long wheelbase Cadillac Special parade car for the King of Saudi Arabia. With ornaments and royal arms of solid gold, the Cadillac was equipped with a radio telephone in the central armrest, plus a bar built into the cupboards behind the front seats. Fitted with pull-out steps for security guards to stand on, this Caddy also had four doors, a rare feature not even used on the Cadillac Eldorado in which President Eisenhower had ridden to his inauguration in January that year.

Marking another historic event of 1953 was a one-off Ghia-MG, the 'Everest', a two-seater convertible built on the classic TF chassis which, with

LEFT ABOVE Another Ghia Abarth sports coupé, this time based on a 1953 Simca Aronde chassis, the first decisive step by this French maker away from its Fiat origins

ABOVE 'Otto Vu'—this beautiful 8V Fiat coupé was shown on the Ghia stand at the 1953 Paris Salon

full-width wings and vestigial tail-fins, achieved the remarkable feat of making the TF look as unexciting as the contemporary Z-Series Magnette.

For Simca, Ghia created an Abarth coupé of pure, flowing lines which seemed to owe more than a little to Exner's 'Firebomb' and 'Firearrow' designs; a similar coupé based on the Fiat-Abarth had a curious 'beak' in the centre of its wide grille which did little for its appearance. Of equally questionable aesthetic value was the front-end treatment of the 1953 Ghia Porsche Spyder, a solid chrome-edged oval with three transverse chrome bars—it looked rather like the loudspeaker opening of an old radio set!

But undoubtedly the event of 1953 as far as Ghia was concerned was the shipping of the first prototype 2 + 2 coupé on the VW Beetle platform from Turin to Wolfsburg. Ghia had already carried out a few design studies for VW, including some 'retouching' of the Beetle's prewar silhouette, but that little coupé was destined to win immortality.

In fact, though Segre claimed responsibility for that VW coupé, recalls Don Kopka, it had really been designed by Virgil Exner, for all Segre had done was to scale down Exner's Chrysler d'Elegance and give it a different front end. Accepted by the VW management, it was put into production as the Karmann-Ghia, starting in 1955: Ghia built maybe 25 Chrysler d'Elegance coupés; at the peak of production, Karmann, a coachbuilding company founded in Osnabruck, Germany, by Wilhelm Karmann in 1901, was turning out 42,000 Ghias annually. A VW convertible designed by Ghia the following year became the Karmann-Ghia VW cabriolet, built from 1957 until the end of 1973; there was also a Karmann-Ghia coupé based on the VW 1500 styled by Sergio Sartorelli and manufactured from 1962–69.

Start of a famous line: this VW cabriolet designed by Ghia for Karmann of Osnabruck in 1954 became the production version of the Karmann Ghia convertible, built from 1957–73

51

Ghia did make one more attempt to produce the d'Elegance concept in quantity with the GS-1, built on the 1954 New Yorker chassis: but only about twenty examples of this coupé, which differed from the d'Elegance in having a Talbot-Lago type of front grille and modified wings, would be constructed by Ghia after the 1954 Paris Salon and sold through the French Chrysler distributor. A few were eventually shipped to the United States.

With its increasing business, Ghia was outgrowing the premises on the via Tommaso Grossi, and in 1954 moved to a plant on the Corso Unione Sovietica. The following year, in an attempt to increase the capacity of Ghia, a new company, Ghia-Monviso-OS, was set up with the stated aims of constructing 'prototypes, one-offs and short run series'; an offshoot company, Ghia Serie Speciali, which had been established in 1952 to customize production coachwork, was also absorbed. With Boano gone, there was a need for new design talent at Ghia, and a series of freelances was hired, among them Michelotti and Frua.

Indeed, there's a minor mystery about Frua's involvement with Ghia, for the Ghia archives include quite a number of photos of Frua bodies—a fact only detectable by examining the prints minutely with a magnifying glass—which suggests that the early Frua bodies may, indeed, have been built in the Ghia workshops. Direct proof, however, does not seem to be forthcoming. . . .

There was also a particularly successful coupé for the luxury 8V Fiat chassis designed by Giovanni Savonuzzi (formerly with Cisitalia); a series of fifty of this _carrozzeria d'avanguardia_ was constructed, and the pure lines of this sporting coupé would reappear on Ghia one-offs on other high-performance chassis during the 1950s.

Since SIATA had helped design the engine of the 8V, it's likely that here, too, the entrepreneurial skills of 'Gigi' Segre had brought new business to Carrozzeria Ghia.

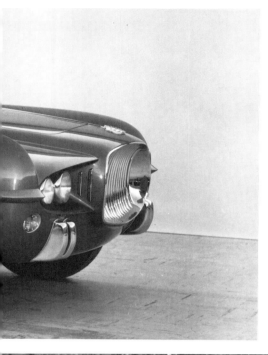

LEFT The Dodge Firearrow sport coupé of 1954, designed by Exner, returned to the quadruple headlamp layout of the prototype: this purposeful-looking two-seater was timed at over 135 mph

BELOW One of the few Ghia bodies of the 1950s that failed to improve on its prototype, the MG-TF 'Everest' roadster of 1953

3 Fins with everything

After the developments of 1953, the following year was one of relative consolidation: the association with Chrysler continued to prove fruitful, for at the Paris Salon, a Chrysler Special was 'the centre of attraction in an exceptionally well-conceived presentation of light and colour'; after the show a series of 20 Chrysler Specials was built especially for the French market.

And as far as Italy was concerned, the most prestigious order came from the Vatican, to construct a special 'throne car' for the Pope on a stretched Chrysler Imperial chassis; the Papal throne was covered by a completely transparent roof and faced by two foldaway opera seats. Unusually, the car didn't carry the crowned Ghia badge, which presumably bore too close a resemblance to the Vatican crests on the rear doors; there was just a discreet cast 'Carrozzeria Ghia Torino' script at the lower rear edge of each front wing.

Working with Alfa Romeo, Ghia turned out a wide and curiously uneven series of designs, ranging from a delightful 1900 Conrero 'Coupé Mille Miglia'—whose two-seater bodywork was obviously derived from that of the Adventurer II, right down to the 'jet-pipe' tail lights—which started as number 453 (for its start time of 4.53 am) in the 1953 Mille Miglia to the most hideously inept hatchback station wagon on the standard 1900 chassis. In between was a two-seater coupé version of the 1900 Sprint with odd concave headlamp housings. A photograph exists in the Ghia archives of Segre explaining this feature to an assembled group of Alfa executives, including Jiri Hruska, who subsequently designed the Alfasud; they look distinctly unimpressed!

There was also an Alfa-Abarth, whose well-balanced lines were, unfortunately, thrown out of kilter by an ill-conceived two-tone colour scheme.

The partnership with Monviso seemed to be off to a good start: besides the production of limited series of small Fiats of the more banal kind, there were some attractive sporting models (which carried the triangular Monviso badge instead of the Ghia shield). Based on the 1100/103, the Monviso Coupé resembled a smaller version of the Ghia-bodied 8V Fiat, while at the 1954 Turin Show the company launched the 1100 cc 'Stella Filante' two-seater sports, which had twin air-scoops in the bonnet and a wrap-around windscreen.

At the end of 1954 came a remarkable demonstration of the work that

LEFT ABOVE Holy See and be seen; this extended-wheelbase Chrysler Imperial limousine was built for Pope Pius XII in 1954

LEFT BELOW Inspired by the Adventurer II, this 1900C Alfa Romeo ran in the 1953 Mille Miglia

LEFT ABOVE In total contrast to the pretty Mille Miglia car overleaf, this overblown 'Giardinetta' estate car was offered on the Alfa 1900 chassis from 1954–58

LEFT BELOW Gigi Segre attempts to explain the front-end styling of his 1900 Alfa Sprint Coupé to Alfa executives: Jiri Hruska (right) looks particularly unimpressed

RIGHT ABOVE Nice car, shame about the paintwork: the elegant lines of this Ghia Alfa Abarth Sport Coupé of 1954 are marred by the strange colour scheme

ABOVE Star of the 1955 Turin Show, the aerodynamic Ghia Gilda, designed by Savonuzzi. Ghia claimed it would reach 140 mph with a dohc 1491 cc OSCA engine fitted, though it seems unlikely that Gilda ever ran under its own power

Ghia had performed for Chrysler: when the corporation opened its new 4000-acre proving ground near Chelsea, Michigan, ten Ghia-built Chrysler dream cars paraded on the oval test track.

Ghia struck out in a new direction in 1955, a 'particularly rich and fortunate year of innumerable projects destined for the other side of the Atlantic'; Savonuzzi had been researching the aerodynamics of car bodies in the wind tunnel at Turin Polytechnic, and it was decided to build a design study that took the imperfectly understood science of vehicle aerodynamics as far as possible. Work began on the project in November 1954, and the dart-shaped dream car, known as 'La Gilda', made its debut at the 1955 Turin Show, where it was the centre of attention.

Rotating gently on its turntable, Gilda looked more like a science-fiction space shuttle than a car. Extremely long, with a bubble cockpit, it had a cuneiform profile terminating in high flared tailfins. The wheels were half-buried in the bodywork, which was constructed of aluminium over a tubular steel frame. After starring in a number of European shows, Gilda was offered free of charge to the Henry Ford Museum in Dearborn; in October 1955 it was shipped to America, where it went on show there.

Nor was Gilda the most sensational 'dream-car' to emerge from the Ghia workshops that year, for the stylists of Lincoln-Mercury had also found their way to Turin, where Ghia's craftsmen interpreted their designs to produce possibly the most bizarre car ever to run on the roads, the Lincoln 'Futura'. Deeply hooded headlamps and a full-width grille gave the front end of the Future the appearance of a myopic sucker-fish, while the body ended in massive fins with dummy air intakes in their forward edge. The occupants sat in twin transparent bubbles; the centre section of the roof swung up to allow entry when the doors were opened.

'The solutions and the automatic devices with which this "dream-car" is equipped have given birth to the definition of a "laboratory on wheels",' enthused *Torino Motori*. 'A dashboard equipped with the most complete instrumentation, which can be totally concealed behind three sliding covers, a steering wheel with speedometer and rev counter in its centre, and a cockpit trimmed in the finest two-coloured leather . . . an exceptional achievement of Italian labour with the real technical honours going to the workers of the Torinese carrozzeria. . . .

The public launch of the Futura was a sensation, for Ford decided not to unveil the car at a motor show, but at a reception in New York's Central Park; the car was driven there through the traffic causing a sensation (and probably a number of minor collisions as disbelieving drivers turned to stare!) A useful accessory was the radio aerial mounted on the boot lid, for it incorporated a microphone which picked up the sound of traffic approaching from the rear.

It took little effort for the strip cartoonists to modify the peculiar lines of the Futura, which were virtually at the level of caricature already, into Batman's 'Batmobile'! And the actual car was transformed into the screen Batmobile by top customizer George Barris: it survives in this form in an American collection of film cars.

And the third of the outstanding Ghia 'dream-cars' of that extraordinary year 1955 represented the dying gasp of the once-great Packard company. As the firm was collapsing under the weight of mounting financial crises,

The original Batmobile! The Ghia-bodied Lincoln Futura caused a sensation when it was launched in 1955, as much as for its bizarre styling as for the ingenious technology it incorporated

it was decided to build a car to show Packard's confidence in the future—and possibly encourage some new investment to enable the company to stagger on for a little longer.

The timetable was as tight as Packard's corporate pursestrings: the car—named 'Predictor' and based on a standard Clipper chassis—had to be built in just 90 days to enable it to appear at the 1956 Chicago Show. Though the Predictor made the show, the rescue operation was unsuccessful.

Contemporary reports claim that though the Predictor was enthusiastically received by the public, dealers and shareholders, its styling, by Richard A. Teague and Dick McAdam, was too restrained to save the company. This opinion seems a trifle fanciful when you look at pictures of the car, which managed to combine just about every tasteless feature that would be seen on American cars in the next few years, like a 'horse-collar' grille à l'Edsel, a reverse-slope rear window, 'opera windows' in the C-pillars, huge and

TOP With the Chrysler A488 Falcon sports two-seater, Exner returned to the external exhaust pipes theme that had featured on the Adventurer I

ABOVE Visibility from the A488 Falcon with the hood up must have been limited; the styling appears to have been shared by Exner and Segre

RIGHT Another Ghia-built Chrysler prototype, this time nearer to production. The Chrysler FliteSweep appeared in 1955; the following year Chrysler and DeSoto cars had sprouted more fins than the Brighton Aquarium

ABOVE LEFT The unspeakable
Plymouth Plainsman built by Ghia
in 1955 seemed to have problems
deciding which way it was going.
And while the occupants were
working it out, the cowhide-covered
seats could be converted electrically
into a double bed . . .

ABOVE RIGHT The Guzzi-powered
Nibbio II record-breaker used
Ghia's aerodynamic expertise to
better 100 mph on 350 cc

LEFT Ghia gigantic—this one-and-a-
half deck Greyhound Scenicruiser
observation bus was built in 1955

63

lethally-pointed tailfins and dual headlamps (hidden behind retractable covers that flipped open just like dolly's eyes!) Features that mercifully remained unique to the Predictor were slide-away panels in the roof that rolled back when the doors opened and swivelling front seats to ease entry.

And of course, there were the Chrysler Corporation concept cars—the Chrysler Berlina ST and A488 Falcon two-seater sports roadster, which returned to the idea of external exhaust pipes, the DeSoto Flite Line and Flight Sweep, which carried their spare wheels in the divided boot lid.

There was also the 'Plainsman', described as 'a station wagon whose lines were at the same time adventurous and classic'; the rear tailgate opened automatically, and two footrests enabled passengers to climb into a third row of seats, set facing across the car. The spare wheel was hidden inside the rear wing, which hinged open to reveal it. But the pièce de résistance was the fact that all the seats (covered in Wild West cowhide) were electrically controlled so that they could be folded down in unison so that 'the entire interior of the car can be transformed at will into one vast double bed!'

As a total contrast, in 1955 Ghia also designed the 'one-and-a-half deck' Scenicruiser luxury coach for the American Greyhound Lines, one of a number of 'gran turismo' coaches they constructed around that time.

Monviso vanished from the scene in 1955; some reports say Ghia absorbed them, others that Casalis severed the link between the two firms. Just to confuse the issue still further, there was a mysterious Swiss subsidiary based in Aigle, near Lausanne. Michelotti apparently worked there—he and Frua were employed by Ghia on a freelance basis after the departure of Boano— but a car-mad Swiss friend who grew up in the Aigle region at that time never came across the Ghia subsidiary, and I've only ever seen one car that they built. It was a rebodied Bugatti Type 57 which, though elegant in the mode of the 1950s, was a very poor substitute for the Jean Bugatti-designed Atalante coachwork that the car wore when new. Uwe Bahnsen of Ford recalls that Ghia-Aigle also built special-bodied Alvis solely for Swiss consumption. The rationale behind the short-lived Swiss subsidiary—it was under Swiss control by 1953—is hard to fathom, unless it merely represented easy access to the land of the numbered bank account. . . .

Again, 1956 was an exceptionally fruitful year for Ghia: the aerodynamic studies which had produced the Gilda were now used to build a tiny record car, 'Nibbio II', powered by a 350 cc Moto Guzzi engine. With Count 'Johnny' Lurani at the wheel, in June 1956 Nibbio II set a new three hour record by covering 393.579 km, an average speed of 131.193 km/h (81.52 mph). Subsequently, driven by Volpini, it broke a number of international records at Monza, averaging some 106 mph in the process.

On a larger scale, the 'Gilda line' was also employed on the Chrysler A-498 'Dart' (also known as the 'Super Gilda'). Recalled Jack Charipar: 'In June of 1955, the Chrysler Corporation began a collaboration with Ghia on an extension of the aerodynamic concepts to a running idea car which would also incorporate the latest structural, power plant and chassis ideas for experimental evaluation and test. . . . The chassis of this car is of advanced design and features a platform frame with experimental suspension, cooling system and power plant.

'The Chrysler Dart has a wheelbase of 10 ft 9 in. and an overall length of 18 ft 9 in. It is 4 ft 6 in. high. I should add that the overall dimensions

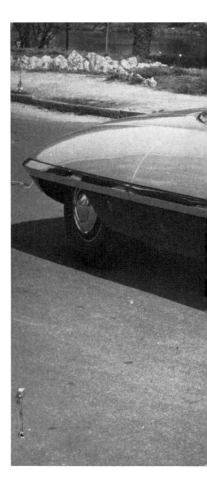

The Chrysler Dart, otherwise known as 'Super Gilda', was based on the Chrysler A498 chassis, with a 375 bhp V8 power unit, and had a retractable metal hardtop. Today, with this novel feature replaced by a fabric hood, the car survives in a Pennsylvania collection

LEFT ABOVE This elegant Sport Coupé on the 375 hp Chrysler chassis was built for the Shah of Persia in 1956

LEFT BELOW Ghia built Chrysler's prototype bodies, too; this 1956 design study photographed in the Ghia courtyard is for the Chrysler 300 'muscle car' series

RIGHT ABOVE The original Chrysler Crown Imperial, at the end of 1956, was this eight-passenger limousine with division

RIGHT BELOW Ghia's interpretation of the Jaguar XK140 appeared in 1956: one wonders what Sir William Lyons thought of it!

LEFT ABOVE With definite overtones of Exner, this Aston Martin DB2/4 Ghia coupé, painted 'an exquisite pale green', starred at the 1956 Turin Show

LEFT CENTRE This 1956 Ghia Berlina Victoria has to be the most sporting Armstrong Siddeley of the postwar era

LEFT BELOW Another 1956 prototype body, this time for a short-wheelbase Crown Imperial A–568 that never made production

RIGHT ABOVE Claimed to be the world's longest convertible, this Ghia Chrysler Crown Imperial was built for Sarabdullah Mubarak Alsabak, Sultan of Kuwait in 1957

RIGHT BELOW The Ford Bimini was supposed to be an estate car for city use; its entire centre section hinged up for easy access in tight parking lots, though if it was pouring with rain, you presumably had to use the tailgate to climb in and out . . .

of this car are actually somewhat smaller than the larger American production cars are at present. Specifically, the Dart is more than $4\frac{1}{2}$ in. shorter than our production Imperials, it is but $\frac{1}{2}$ in. longer than our production Windsor and New Yorker series, and $2\frac{1}{2}$ in. shorter than the larger Cadillacs.'

Powered by a K300 V8 engine developing some 375 bhp, the Dart had light alloy panelling over a steel frame; the doors were in steel and, when shut, were positively locked into the structure, which was said to be exceptionally rigid. The roof was in steel, too, and could be electrically retracted into the rear compartment whether the car was stationary or in motion; with the roof closed, the Dart was said to have a drag coefficient of only 0.17. Repainted and slightly modified—its fins have been docked—the car still exists today, though it now goes under the name of 'Diablo'.

There was even a 'Gilda line' Ferrari, a 410 Superamerica coupé with high rear fins, built to the order of Bob Wilke of Wisconsin; Ford designer Manfred Lampe, who liaises with Ghia, has described it as 'dramatic, but not very fitting for a Ferrari chassis'.

Dramatic, too, was the Chrysler Special K-300 built that year for the Shah of Persia; 'indubitably one of the most luxurious cars yet built', with radio telephone, refrigerator, long-playing gramophone and air-conditioning, the Chrysler was remarkably well-proportioned for such a huge, low-slung car— it was nearly 20 ft long and over 7 ft wide—though that year Ghia built an even bigger car for the Sultan of Kuwait, Sarabdullah Mubarak Alsabak. That was a four-door convertible Chrysler Crown Imperial, 'the world's longest car'; it was equipped not only with a 'Highway Hi-Fi' but also a short-wave two-way radio. Another special Crown Imperial was built for

Ghia grandiose: another bus design from the Torinese studio, this time a Gran Turismo Leyland Royal Tiger

the King of Saudi Arabia, with a double roof for protection against the heat of the sun and armour-plating for protection against assassins' bullets. With retractable footrests for the royal guards to ride on, it was upholstered in velvet and precious hides and carried solid gold crests.

A later commission for the Saudi monarch was a 'hunting car' which, apart from the giant 'cookie-cutter' crown motif in the centre of the radiator grille, looked like a normal, if super-long, Chrysler convertible with the hood erect. But the transformation was dramatic: the windscreen unclipped, and was housed on special mountings on the boot lid, the rear seat rose high on hydraulic rams so that the bold hunters could shoot over the head of the driver, and hunting rifles were revealed in racks carried on the rear doors!

In total contrast was a series of three closed sports bodies built on British chassis, two of them streamlined coupés on the Jaguar XK140 and Aston Martin DB2 respectively and the third a 'Berlina Victoria' based on Ghia's Ferrari Inter Berlinetta; remarkably, this handsome sporting saloon was built on that least sporting of marques, the Armstrong Siddeley. . . .

The year 1956 also saw the culmination of 15 months' work on a remarkable dream car, the Chrysler Norseman, 'the world's most automatic car', designed by Virgil Exner and Bill Brownlie. The most immediately noticeable feature of the Norseman was its cantilever roof, 'the fruit of profound studies of the resistance of material and of its load-bearing qualities', which enabled Ghia to dispense with the normal A-pillars, and thus give the driver all-round vision.

Moreover, the rear window could be retracted electrically into the roof and the headlamps were concealed behind hinged eyelids which popped open

Gallic bone of contention: though Ghia had designed the Renault Floride, Frua also claimed responsibility, and a lawsuit ensued. This is the second prototype on the line at Flins, 2 December, 1958

thanks to complex camplates. Inside, access to the rear seats was made easier by front seatbacks which revolved electrically about their vertical axis (and which could be operated by remote control); all four seats were adjustable in all directions so that the passengers could choose the anatomical position best suited to their physique. Lap seat belts which retracted into the transmission tunnel were another advanced feature; but all that creative effort had been in vain, for the decision had been taken to ship the Norseman to America aboard the *Andrea Doria*. And on July 26, 1956, when the Italian liner foundered off North Carolina, all that automation (it had cost 45 million lire to build) went to the bottom of the Atlantic: Exner and Brownlie never saw their creation. They did, however, receive the prototype bodyshells created by Ghia for the Imperial A-568 and the A-613, then crated and shipped to America to be put into series production.

Chrysler had determined that Ghia's craftsmanship would enable them to get back into the luxury car field and compete with Cadillac, which held 90 per cent of the limousine market, without incurring the cost of the special tooling which would make the production of a luxury variant of the all-new 1957 K-series Imperial prohibitively expensive to manufacture in America. Once the decision had been made to go ahead, Chrysler placed an initial order with Ghia for 25 eight-passenger limousines with division, to be delivered between November 1956 and May 1957.

All the design work was carried out in America; styling was by Virgil Exner, aided by Bill Brownlie and Cliff Voss, while the chief engineer was Jack Charipar, with Dave Cohoe as Ghia coordinator and Paul Farago

LEFT ABOVE Jolly time had by all? This is the 1954 Ghia Jolly conversion of the Renault 4CV

LEFT BELOW And this is the 1957 Lambretta Jolly (Ghia had also styled the Lambretta scooter)

RIGHT BELOW And this is the archetypal Jolly, based on the Fiat 600. The woven plastic interior of this 1962 Jolly has been retouched over the original cane seats

LEFT ABOVE A specially-lengthened Ghia Mercedes cabriolet, built for an Arab customer in 1956

LEFT CENTRE One of Virgil Exner's least appealing Ghia prototypes, the 1958 Chrysler Imperial D'Elegance, developed the stylistic theme of the ill-fated Norseman

ABOVE Two views of Tom Tjaarda's curious 1959 Selene I, which ended its days in Moscow

LEFT BELOW This last-ditch Ghia-built 1956 prototype Packard was called the Predictor; all the styling trends it predicted were visual disasters

LEFT ABOVE Virgil Exner Jr was responsible for the 1962 Selene II, an engineless mockup

LEFT BELOW Picking up the Selene theme was this grotesque Renault 900 prototype of 1959

ABOVE Exner's overblown 1961 Dodge FliteWing was powered by a 6276 cc V8

TOP Tom Tjaarda's dragster, the IXG, was too streamlined to take its Innocenti power plant

resident engineer in Turin. A close friend of Exner and Segre, Farago was a well-known builder of sports-racing cars who had run a leading car importing agency near Detroit before becoming Ghia's representative in America at the time of the Chrysler K-310. American by birth and Italian by background, Farago spoke good Italian and worked well with Ghia's craftsmen; his job in Turin was to oversee the construction of the wooden framing over which the sheet metal could be formed, and the manufacture of jigs and fittings.

Ghia, in fact, was to build the entire car from a kit shipped from Detroit consisting of a 129-in. wheelbase Imperial Convertible chassis (chosen because of its extra cross-bracing) carrying a two-door Imperial hardtop coupé in primer, less doors, seats and glass, and fitted with oversize tyres. Also packed were sill panels, front and rear sedan doors and centre pillars (all were modified by Ghia), seat frames ready for trimming, wiring looms, electric window mechanisms, heating and air-conditioning units, paint and trim materials and special mechanical components like a longer propeller shaft.

On arrival in Turin, the body and chassis were cut in two and extended by 20.5 in., with new floor and sill panels made by Ghia. A new roof panel incorporating cutouts for the extended doors was fitted, along with new framing and ducting for the air conditioning. Once the bodyshell had been stretched and assembled, it was hand finished: not a joint or seam was allowed to show, even inside the doors! To that end, some 150 lb of body leading was used on each car.

Up to 17 hours were spent on hanging the doors and wings, adjusting the fit of all sheet metal parts to a maximum gap of 4 mm. The entire body was then acid-etched and primed with zinc-chromate paint, followed by a black undercoat which has allowed to dry, then sanded to reveal low spots in the panelling, which were then filled and sanded.

Successive colour coats—standard colours were black, dark green, dark blue and maroon—were applied and sanded. Finally, the body was rubbed down with an ultra-fine sandpaper, then buffed up with a solution of water and sepia (obtained from cuttlefish) to bring the paint to a mirror finish before the cream coach stripe was applied.

Glass and exterior trim—mostly pull-ahead 1958 items on the 1957 cars—were then fitted, and the interior trimmed in top quality broadcloth, with fine woods, glove-trade leather, hand finished metal mouldings and sheared mouton carpeting. The driver's seat was finished in narrow-pleated black leather, with black nylon carpet on the floor (and in the boot).

That initial order for 25 cars was extended into an association that was to last until 1964, though the biggest batch of Crown Imperials—36 cars—was built in the first year, and over half of them had been manufactured during the first two years. It took Ghia about a month to build one Crown Imperial, of which two weeks were taken up with paint and trim.

The finished car would be taken out for a somewhat uncritical road test: the tyres were inflated to a rock-hard 40 lb/sq. in. and the car was driven over cobbled streets to see if anything rattled or fell off. On return to the Ghia works, it was boxed for shipment; Ghia's packing crates were apparently of such high quality that on one occasion a train carrying a Ghia Crown Imperial across the desert for delivery to an Arab sheik was hijacked by

RIGHT Series-production Ghia bodies were most often seen on the Fiat 2300S; this, however, is a Fiat 2100S Ghia Coupé

BELOW A Ghia-bodied Chrysler Crown Imperial built for the White House in 1959 carries the American Eagle on bonnet and doors

desert bandits, who unpacked the Chrysler and stole its crate!

The finished cars were taken in their crates by truck to Genoa for shipping to New York, whence they were taken to Detroit for final road testing and inspection; from start to finish the building of the Ghia Crown Imperial had taken about six months, and the cars sold for around $12,000 in New York.

Crown Imperials were sold, apart from those Arab monarchs, to RCA head David Sarnoff, novelist Pearl S. Buck, Mrs Anna Dodge, Governor Nelson Rockefeller of New York and the White House. And one Crown Imperial, specially fitted with a raised rear seat and transparent bubble-dome, was used by Queen Elizabeth II and Prince Philip for their tour of Canada in 1959.

Also produced for America in 1956 was the curious Ford Bimini estate car, a paradoxical creation designed for operation in crowded urban conditions; instead of doors, the entire forward portion of the cabin tilted forward, lifting the steering wheel with it, allowing the Bimini to be parked in a space no wider than the car. The utility of this, however, was questionable in bad weather, for the front seats were completely exposed to the elements when the lid was lifted. The other space-saving idea of the Bimini was that all the seats could be folded down to form an immense load-carrying platform: 'for what is essentially a working vehicle, the lines are well balanced and the aesthetic solutions not inferior to other luxury solutions,' thought _Torino Motori_.

At the other end of the size scale came an _autobus da gran turismo_ on a

LEFT ABOVE The unlikely face of equality: a Volga Ghia design study of 1960

LEFT BELOW Another red revolution: Ghia proposed this cleaned-up version of the Moskvitch 407 in 1962

BELOW A Ghia-built prototype Chrysler, the Plymouth 250 Valiant fastback, dating from 1959

TOP & CENTRE Plymouth XNR 'Assimetrica' almost made production; instead, this prototype was bought by a Genevan butcher, who sold it to the Shah of Persia

ABOVE This more polished 'Assimetrica' was based on a Chrysler Falcon; Maigret's creator Georges Simenon bought it

Designed by Maury Baldwin, the Chrysler Turboflite was driven by a CR2A gas turbine and featured a lift-up canopy and moveable rear aerofoil. It was one of the last showcars built for Virgil Exner by Ghia

ABOVE This curious little device was a 1961 Ghia design for a go-kart!

LEFT Another miniature Ghia oddity; this Ferbedo 'Automobilina' pedal car was designed by Tom Tjaarda in 1961

TOP RIGHT Pioneering sports hatchback, the Fiat 2300S Club was produced by Ghia-OSI and featured at the Turin Show in 1962

RIGHT This curious 1964 R8 sports coupé was one of many design studies carried out by Ghia for Renault in the early 1960s

Leyland Royal Tiger chassis; like the mopeds, scooters, fridges and washing machines styled by Ghia at this period, it was evidence that Ghia was not just a designer and builder of car bodies. Indeed, some quite utilitarian small Fiats were constructed, as was a notably ill-proportioned design study for a small van on the Volkswagen chassis; unladen, from the rear, it had a ludicrously bandy-legged appearance thanks to VW's swing axles.

That, however, was one of the few failures in Ghia's programme of design studies for outside companies: on the positive side were commissions for Renault, for whom Ghia designed the Floride (though there was some disagreement with Frua, who also claimed responsibility for the design, an argument that eventually led to litigation) and for Volvo.

For the Gothenburg company who, save for the excessively curious 'aerodynamic' Venus Bilo of 1935, had an unbroken record of pedestrian styling, Ghia created a classic coupé, the P1800, which achieved fame as the *Saint*'s car in the long running British television detective series.

Ghia also produced various series of 'Jolly' cars, mostly on small Fiat chassis—500, 600 and 600 Multipla—but also on the 4CV Renault; these were open vehicles with cane bench seats, which a tri-lingual leaflet described as 'the ideal little car for *Your* amusement with *Your* friends and for *Your* tourist trips.' The concept of the Jolly was odd enough; the Lambretta Jollys of 1957 were downright crazy, consisting of those cane bench seats across the back of a Lambretta *triporteur* to create a motorized rickshaw intended for Far Eastern markets. Curious though the Lambretta Jolly was, it seems as though, since Ghia had designed the original Lambretta, they felt that if anyone had to gild that particular lily, then it ought to be themselves. . . .

Ghia moved again in 1957, taking over premises in the via Agostino de Montefeltro formerly occupied by a small steel milling and laminating company in order to increase output. At this time, a number of Ghia creations appeared for which the company perhaps shouldn't be blamed, for they were only carrying out orders. Like the 1959 Chrysler Imperial d'Elegance, an overbodied befinned behemoth of squaloid infelicity, and a rare lapse of taste for Virgil Exner.

The company was also undertaking limited production for Dual Motors, a Detroit haulage contractors headed by one Gene Casaroll, who had the idea of building limited edition luxury cars with Chrysler power. Casaroll's company shipped Chrysler D-500 chassis to Ghia, where they were fitted with special coachwork derived from the 1953 Firebomb. Prices started from $7646, and the cars were available either as hardtop or convertible; in both guises they came equipped with PowerFlite automatic transmission, radio, heater and English leather upholstery.

The first series of Dual Ghias appeared in 1956, the second around 1958, when the price had soared to $18,000. Production of both series was just over 100 cars, but the reason for the cessation of Dual Ghia production wasn't due to a shortage of people who could afford Dual Ghias, but to a rash of warranty work. Filippo Sapino, who entered the Ghia drawing office around 1960 as a young designer, explained why: 'It started with the first Dual Ghia. It was crated up and shipped to Detroit, and when it was uncrated, the president of Chrysler was there to examine this exciting new car. He grabbed the door handle and pulled—and the door fell off and nearly chopped off his foot!'

'But the cars just hadn't been built for road use. The workmen didn't

LEFT ABOVE A Ghia clay proposal for Renault's project 112 small car, circa 1960

LEFT BELOW Another full-size prototype built for Renault by Ghia, the 1963 Project 115 Ontario was a two-door coupé version of the Renault 16, due to appear in 1965

87

understand that these cars were going to be operated over all types of high-way. They had used plenty of body filler to get the smooth lines of the Dual Ghias just right; so that when the cars were driven on rough roads, the filler dropped off in lumps!'

So much for the Dual company's rash slogan: 'Rolls Royce is the car of those who cannot afford a Dual Ghia. . .'. Nevertheless, the Dual Ghia was a favourite with Hollywood's 'Rat Pack'; Frank Sinatra, Sammy Davis Jr and Dean Martin all owned Dual Ghias.

Coachwork by Ghia was tops with dictators, too: Peron, Sukarno and Tito all came to the Torinese *carrozzeria* for their state vehicles, overblown tourers of inordinate length. Tito, for instance, had a four-door convertible Cadillac Eldorado, surely one of the most arrogantly capitalistic cars ever to carry the Red Star (albeit discreetly, on its Serbian numberplate). And a Crown Imperial was sold to Rafael Trujillo, dictator of Dominica, whose family would soon figure large in the Ghia story.

During 1958, a Finnish design professor working in the United States at the University of Michigan met Luigi Segre, who offered to train the professor's most promising young designer at Ghia. The choice fell on a young architectural student of Dutch extraction named Tom Tjaarda, whose father, John, had headed the Briggs Motor Bodies studio in Detroit in the 1930s and been responsible for the streamlined and futuristic Sterkenberg that had caused a stir in the design contest held as part of the 1933 Chicago Century of Progress Exposition. John Tjaarda had then gone on to design the classic Lincoln-Zephyr of the 1930s.

Today, Tom Tjaarda heads a Turin design studio called Dimensione Design, but his recollections of his days at Ghia are still vivid: 'Though I had trained as an architect, I'd designed cars for fun ever since I was in school. However, I'd never dreamed I would ever become a car designer, so when my professor asked me if I'd like to work with Ghia in Turin after I graduated, it was the impossible dream come true!'

'I just got a ticket for the boat and came over to Europe and arrived in Italy. The arrangement was that I would work in Turin for six months to a year. That was 25 years ago—and I'm still here!'

During his first stint with Ghia, which lasted from 1959–61, Tom Tjaarda created a couple of famous 'dream cars', the Selene I and the IXG.

Selene—the name is that of the Greek moon goddess—was 'an experimental realization and innovatory solution for a near tomorrow'. Covered by a whole pile of international patents, the Selene was an engineless full-size design study for a car of unusual configuration: the driving seats, the steering wheel could be swung in front of either seat, were ahead of the front wheels.

'It is,' claimed Ghia 'a true comfort to have a car with left and right drive at the same time, according to the personal preferences and the opportunities and requirements of use . . . for current use in town, for touring on country roads or on mountain roads with curves!'

Odd and impractical though it was, the Selene's fame was widespread; Segre received a letter from the University of Moscow which said that they were carrying out studies for the design of a taxicab, and that the Selene was exactly the kind of vehicle they were investigating. So Selene was duly shipped to Moscow once its show life was over; some years later, Tom

LEFT The Mark I Karmann Ghia Coupé was styled by Luigi Segre with a good deal of inspiration from Virgil Exner, and was built by Karmann in Osnabruck, Germany between 1956–74

BELOW This aggressive-looking Cadillac Eldorado convertible was built by Ghia as a state vehicle for President Tito of Yugoslavia

ABOVE Though Exner had left Chrysler in 1961, Ghia still built some design studies for the Detroit corporation, like this Plymouth Valiant-based 'St. Regis' completed in August 1962

LEFT ABOVE The sleek Fiat 1100TV coupé was another Ghia-OSI series-produced model of the early 1960s

LEFT The astounding Chrysler hunting car built for the King of Saudi Arabia in 1961: with hood down and screen clipped on the bootlid, hunters on the elevated rear seat had a clear field of fire!

Tjaarda was surprised to receive some photographs of a Moscow taxi that was obviously inspired by his Selene, but ineptly executed: 'It was *horrible*!'

Nor were the Russians the only people to find inspiration in the unorthodox layout of Selene, for Renault also commissioned a series of design studies for a 'Renault 900', a curious rear-engined 'people-mover' which only succeeded in looking horrific, and seemed to use up more space by adopting the Selene's forward control layout than it would have done had it been front-engined!

A 'Selene Seconda' came along a year or two later, but Tjaarda had nothing to do with it; this time, the Selene was the work of Virgil Exner Jr, and still survives in the little collection of historic Ghia cars preserved at the factory. A bubble-topped three seater, Selene II was again an engineless dummy, though it was designed to be rear engined, and had a central driving position with aircraft-like controls; the rear-facing passenger seats were furnished with a television screen!

Tom Tjaarda's other 1959 flight of fancy was the IXG: 'Segre had seen drag racing, and was enthused with the idea of building a "dragster" to take records powered by a 950 cc Innocenti engine.' Tjaarda, however, let the beautifully-contoured design run away with him to such an extent that when the car was built it was incapable of taking the intended power train: 'If we'd fitted that engine, it would have stuck up right through the hood!' When Segre discovered that the IXG —the name signified 'Innocenti & Ghia—was a non-runner, he flew into a tremendous paroxysm of rage; the walls of the plant really shook that day!

The episode of the Dual-Ghia had proved that the company was really not capable of undertaking even modest series production; but now Segre had shown two handsome new body designs by Tom Tjaarda to Fiat—the 2300S coupé and Innocenti, the 950 spider, and secured contracts to build these cars in quantity.

In order to obtain the space and finance to undertake these contracts, Segre sought assistance from the Olivetti business machine company; as a result, a new corporation was established jointly by Ghia and Fergat, a stamping and wheel-making company owned by Olivetti. The new firm, based just across the via Agostino de Montefeltro from Ghia, was called OSI; the initials stood for 'Officine Stampaggi Industriali' (Industrial Stamping Company), though cynics said they really signified Olivetti Segre Innocenti. . . .

With a fully paid up capital of 275 million lire, OSI 'entered the automotive industry in a specially favourable and lively period of the national and world economic life'. The corporation's president was Arrigio Olivetti, while Segre was managing director; its plant covered 21,000 sq. m and incorporated two continuous-loop production lines, with provision for a third, plus a 780 m long paint line. It employed some 600 people and could turn out approximately 50 cars a day. Apart from variations on the Fiat 2300S—the convertible was described as a 'car of great luxury for the discerning motorist: a slight rustling sound and the hood opens and closes; just a touch, and the windows raise and lower . . . a convertible for those who want to be elegant at all seasons'. OSI also produced 1300 and 1500 Fiats, plus the Innocenti 950 Spider.

Alongside this expansion into quantity production, Ghia continued its work as a design studio, styling the Chrysler 300 and New Yorker, then,

in 1960 came another joint venture with Chrysler, the L 6.4 ('Luxury that moves with you!')

The company spared no hyperbole in promoting the L 6.4: 'The luxury that surrounds you in the Ghia L 6.4 can only flow from the unhurried hands of dedicated craftsmen, dedicated towards one end . . . to create an automobile that is virtually the next best to "one of a kind". Yes, at Ghia the word "custom" still means individual attention to every detail of styling, construction . . . faithful application of experience gathered from producing the personal automobiles of the most discriminating clientele in the world!' They were, perhaps, on more shaky ground when they claimed: 'The unprecedented demand created by the Dual Ghia has more than been answered by its distinguished successor, the Ghia L 6.4.'

However, they then attempted to redeem the situation by adding: 'Every operating convenience has been incorporated into this exciting new car . . . every luxury to delight the eye and to pamper quality-conscious owners has been lavished upon it!'

The lessons learned from the unfortunate Dual Ghia episode had obviously been taken to heart, for the company claimed that 'to ensure maximum, trouble-free performance from the moment of delivery, each car is subjected to an exhaustive 500 mile road test, after which the car qualifies for its six-month guarantee!'

But alas for those claims that the car was built to 'satisfy machines of precision measurement', for Filippo Sapino recalls: 'If you checked those luxury cars, you would find a dramatic asymmetry between the two sides— there could be as much as an inch variation from side to side!'

Another series produced car to emanate from OSI was historic in marking the first quantity manufacture of a Ford car bearing the Ghia badge. When the new 105E Anglia had reached Italy, the head of Ford Italiana, the magically-named Filmer M. Paradise, decided he didn't care for the distinctive reverse slope rear window devised by stylist Colin MacGregor, and that a more conventional design would sell better on the local market.

So he approached Ghia, and asked them to design and build an Anglia with a 'positive' slope to the rear window. The task was handed to a team

ABOVE Another anonymous Ghia Porsche saloon dating from 1962

TOP An earlier Ghia Porsche: this rather portly 1500 cc Spyder was built in 1953

ABOVE RIGHT Strange attempt on an Alfa Romeo 1900 chassis same time in 1962. Are those actually vents around the headlamps

RIGHT A mysterious Ghia design study for a three-wheeler, apparently jet-propelled, dating from 1961

which now included the 'new recruit', Sapino: 'When we were presented with the design theme, it quickly became apparent that it was impossible to create a "normal" car. As soon as you tried to give the Anglia a normal rear window, it looked like a Moskvitch! The job was given to Michelotti: I admit the Anglia Torino he produced looked better, but he wasn't proud of it!'

There were other curious commissions for cosmetic surgery about which Ghia maintains a low retrospective profile: a Morris Isis estate car, a Warszawa, a Moskvitch and a Volga; in every case, the basic concept of the car was so ill-proportioned that it defied beautification!

Back in 1959, Ghia had built an odd Exner-designed Plymouth sports car, the 'XNR', in which the two halves of the car were asymmetrical, a massive bulge over the offset engine adding to the oddly imbalanced effect. Exner claimed he was 'striving to avoid the static and bulky, which is ugly, and not what an automobile should look like.' Certainly the car's 'graceful look, with a built-in feeling of motion' appealed to a Genevan butcher, who was the XNR's first owner, though Exner later recalled that it found its way into the hands of the Shah of Persia in 1968–69, then turned up in Kuwait in 1972.

A more polished road-going version of Exner's 'Asimmetrica' appeared in 1961, built on a Chrysler Valiant chassis: its appearance was very much an acquired taste, but it was one which appealed to the French detective writer Georges Simenon, who bought the car on the spot!

There was another wondrously impractical commission for Chrysler in 1961: the Corporation had determined to build the world's first series-production gas turbine car, and commissioned Ghia to build it. The Turboflite of 1961 was the advance guard of the series production, a 'dream car' of frighteningly aggressive appearance whose rectilinear front wings left the wheels exposed. Designed by Maury Baldwin, who thought it 'one of the best engineered cars we ever did', the Turboflite had a 'bubble top' that lifted automatically on stalks as soon as the doors were opened; a hint of things to come was the rear spoiler, carried on tall fins like the tailplane of a jet aircraft. It rotated to act as an airbrake!

Ghia also built the production run of 50 Chrysler gas turbine cars, which had more conventional passenger accommodation, though the bold experiment failed to end with public acceptance of the jet car concept, and at the conclusion of the test programme in 1966, all but ten of the Ghia-built Chrysler jet cars were broken up.

And to prove that Ghia was truly operating as a design studio catering for all segments of the automotive industry, 1961 saw the building of a streamlined go-kart as well as a prototype *automobilina* designed by Tom Tjaarda for a company called Ferbedo. Again the means of propulsion were somewhat unorthodox: the Ferbedo was a child's pedal car, and if that sole Ferbedo could be located today, would be even more collectable than its near-contemporary, the Austin pedal car. . . .

At the beginning of the 1960s, a young executive named Giacomo Gaspardo Moro joined Ghia as Segre's personal assistant: Gaspardo Moro, who today lives in the Turin suburb of Pino Torinese, told me how Ghia operated in those days: 'I joined Ghia the day after Easter 1960 as assistant to the president, Luigi Segre. We had built prototypes and were preparing

ABOVE A handsome Ghia Maserati 3500GT coupé built in 1961

RIGHT Dated in the early 1960s was the 500 based 'Ziba'. Neat, possibly useful, but no competition for the scooter-trike commercials

a small series of the Innocenti 950 that were to be built at OSI. We were also working on the pre-series of the Fiat 2300 coupé. We built the prototypes and the first ten or 15 cars at Ghia, and then produced the cars in series at OSI across the road. We built a small series of the 1500 Fiat coupé, I remember. Ghia OSI built about five of those a day. There were prototypes for Ford and Chrysler—and continuous collaboration with Renault.'

Among the fruits of the latter relationship were design studies for the boxy Renault R4, and for a super-streamlined Gordini sports coupé based on the eccentrically angular R8. It was a period when Renault's design was almost idiosyncratically Gallic, yet Billancourt felt it necessary to temper its stylistic chauvinism with the Italian expertise of Ghia.

'Of course,' continued Gaspardo Moro, 'we were still building the show cars and the luxurious special models—I remember an order from an Arab king for a hunting Cadillac.

'It wasn't difficult working with these important people—once the design had been agreed, they didn't change much. It was just a question of altering small details. I do recall one order, though, where we thought the colour they wanted the limousine painted wasn't suitable, and suggested some alternatives, which were refused. They insisted on the car being painted pink—it was for the Royal concubines!'

But the pace was telling on Segre: on one of his trips to America in February 1963, he complained of feeling tired, and went into the Henry Ford Hospital in Detroit for a check-up. The doctors told him that not only was he suffering from gall bladder trouble, but that he should have his appendix removed as soon as possible.

Though the news must have been a shock to him, Segre continued with his business trip, but arranged to go into the city's leading hospital, where a friend would perform the operation, directly on his return to Turin.

Five days later, he died under the anaesthetic, aged only 44.

'Segre was an interesting, dynamic man who travelled much,' said Gaspardo Moro. 'He was a man who saw far. He was the best coachbuilder—the first one from Turin to do business with the United States. Thanks to the Karmann-Ghia models built for America, for many years Ghia was better known in the United States than Pinin Farina!

'I remember the first time I arrived at Kennedy Airport, there was a sign advertising "Karmann-Ghia Automobiles". Ghia was famous in the whole automobile field in the United States. And it was all due to Gigi Segre. He was an exceptional man!

'The death of Segre was crucial to the history of Ghia, for it occurred at a period when all the most important companies like Pinin Farina and Bertone were being transformed from artisanal companies to industrialized companies. But at Ghia, Segre had died; nobody was interested in transforming Ghia from its artisanal stage into an industrialized one, so Ghia stayed small. . . .'

To fill the void left by Segre's death, Gaspardo Moro asked his friend Gino Rovere to take over the running of the company. 'Rovere was a very important man in the automobile field. He worked for Ford in Italy, and was a personal friend of Henry Ford. He lived in Rome, and was president of UNRAE—that's the organization that represents foreign automobile companies who import into Italy. He had many contacts in Europe and America—that's why I invited him to join Ghia.'

The Italian influence has thankfully resumed control in this Chrysler V280 prototype featured on the Ghia stand at the 1964 Turin Show

Count Gino Rovere was indeed a significant figure in the motoring world, and not just because of his industry contacts. Back in the mid-1930s, he had run the Scuderia Sub-Alpina, established by Maserati as a rival to the Scuderia Ferrari. A 'gentleman driver' who had appeared at Brooklands at the wheel of a Maserati, Rovere numbered 'Phi-Phi' Etancelin, Giuseppe Farina (nephew of Pinin) and Geofredo Zehender in his team, which competed valiantly in 1935–36, but was outclassed by its opposition. 'Unfortunately, Rovere was already ill when he came to Ghia, and after only one year, he died.'

Before that, OSI had been hived off (it still operates across the road from Ghia) and ownership of Ghia had changed hands; in September 1963, Segre's widow, the Contessa Louise Segre, sold 75 per cent of the shares to Leonidas Ramadas Trujillo, son of the recently deposed dictator of Dominica. Having fled into exile with a considerable fortune, Trujillo Junior had set up home in France and was investing in racehorses.

The Trujillos had a keen interest in high performance cars: General Rafael Trujillo was an early customer for a Pegaso Z–102 with flamboyant Touring bodywork. Since he had also owned a Chrysler Ghia Crown Imperial, his son would obviously have been familiar with the skills of the Torinese carrozzeria.

Filippo Sapino has a clear memory of the sale to Trujillo: 'I was on military service, and I was called in to the commanding officer and told that Ghia had requested that I be given special leave to return to the factory. It seems as though they wanted to put everything they had in the window to show Trujillo when he was considering buying the company. I didn't mind the leave, but I did feel like a horse in a sale when we all had to line up for Trujillo to inspect us!'

Trujillo, it seems, paid a total of $3 million for control of Ghia, but only visited the company once a year, and then only for an hour or so. 'For Trujillo,' recalls Gaspardo Moro, 'Ghia was a *divertissement*!' That's borne out by the fact that Trujillo never employed his new acquisition to build him a personal car, which would have been, one feels, only natural: 'But we did design him some wine labels!' says Sapino.

Under the control of such an absentee landlord, the continuity that Segre had so carefully built up was broken. 'Under Segre,' comments Filippo Sapino, 'Ghia was dealing with the major manufacturers. After he died, the situation evolved steadily. Gaspardo Moro tried hard to create new initiatives and to carry on as if nothing had changed, but Ghia was rapidly running out of work.'

One link that was broken by Segre's death was the Chrysler connection: since 1959, when only seven Ghia Crown Imperials were sold, output had anyway been minimal. Sixteen were sold in 1960, nine in 1961 and none

RIGHT The Ford 'Clan' concept car was built by Ghia on a Falcon base in the spring of 1964

LEFT Shown at Turin in October
1964, the 'G 230 S' was a sports
coupé based on the Fiat 2300S

at all the following year. In 1963, Chrysler sold 13 Ghia Crown Imperials, which Ghia built alongside those 50 turbine cars. Twenty more cars were built in 1964, of which half remained unsold until the following year, when they were facelifted with a 1965 grille.

Chrysler discontinued the Ghia programme, and had the tooling for the limousines shipped to their Spanish subsidiary Barreiros, where a further ten Ghia Crown Imperials were built for 'chiefs of state and other emirs'. Two were delivered by Eduardo Barreiros to Generalissimo Franco, who owned them until his death in the mid-1970s. The Caudillo and his family used the armour-plated cars for long journeys, particularly for holiday trips to Galicia, to his Palace of Ayete or to the mountains. Franco's holiday processions consisted of nine to 14 cars, plus 16 motorcycle outriders, bowling along at an average speed of some 60 mph.

One of Franco's Ghia Chryslers, a 7.2 litre Imperial LeBaron said to have cost a million pesetas to build, was left to his favourite niece, Carmen Martinez-Bordiu, who still owned it in 1984, when she was reported to be offering it for sale. The other, reputed to have been a present from General de Gaulle to Franco, is owned today by Sara Montiel, a Spanish film star known as 'Spain's Mae West', who has replaced the sober broadcloth upholstery with gold lamé fabric. From new, the car was fitted with a television set, bar and telephone (though the present owner has removed the 'phone in the search for privacy).

Sapino recalls one of those attempts to find new work in the confused months following Segre's death: 'Lamborghini appeared at exactly the time that Rovere showed up and almost immediately disappeared. We did some work for them, because Lamborghini had built his first car and was not very pleased with the design. It had been made by Scaglione, who had originally been the head of design at Bertone and had become a freelance. As a freelance he had designed this car for Lamborghini, who was not happy with it. So he came to us and asked for a redesign. But though we made some renderings, the car was never built.

'It was a strange period of time when I believe Gaspardo Moro was desperately trying to find new customers. After a while he began accepting commissions from less important manufacturers.' Nevertheless, though it was in some ways an unsatisfactory situation, the Trujillo years did see some interesting developments for Ghia.

'Up to then, whenever Ghia had been offered work by the Japanese, it had been rejected. The company attitude was that even though the Japanese had only a small presence in Europe then, we shouldn't trust them—it was felt that they would just copy everything. . . .'

In 1964, however, Ghia did at last succumb to the blandishments of the mystic East, and took on work for Isuzo of Tokyo. The company produced a number of designs for the new Bellett saloon, though they were working with somewhat unpromising material. That year, too, came a commission from a small racing-car builder from the south side of Modena, De Tomaso Automobili, which in its short life (it was founded in 1959), had built some ingenious, but unsuccessful designs—like a racing car chassis with suspension arms made of flexible metal.

The founder of that nine-man company, Alejandro de Tomaso, was to completely change the course of Ghia's history. . . .

4 Don't cry for De T, Argentina

Turin's Tre Colonne restaurant, just down the road from Ghia, is a meeting place for the motor industry. The party at the next table may be members of the Maserati family or Ford executives visiting Ghia. On the eve of the 1984 Turin Salon, the restaurant, with its elegant wood panelling and walls hung with original paintings was crowded, its diners conversing in a babble of tongues. One party of five or six people stood out: 'Isn't that Bertocchi of Maserati?' asked a British television presenter hosting his team for dinner as the little group stood up to leave. But it wasn't the executives of Maserati and Innocenti who were the focus of attention: obviously the dominant member of the group was a short, grey-haired man wearing a camel overcoat, with a canary-yellow woollen shawl about his shoulders. He emanated power in that almost tangible way that is peculiar to Italian businessmen; he was instantly recognizable as Alejandro de Tomaso, owner of Maserati and Innocenti as well as two of Italy's leading motorcycle companies, friend of the great Giovanni Agnelli of Fiat and one-time head of Ghia and Vignale.

Though he was born in Buenos Aires in 1928, De Tomaso was only one generation removed from his Italian origins; his father was active in Argentinian politics as a parliamentary representative, but died when Alejandro was only five years old. His mother came from a well-connected Spanish family, descendants of the viceroys who governed Argentina in the 16th Century, and substantial landholders in the regions to the north of Buenos Aires.

Before he was 20, young Alejandro was running these estates, but determined to break out of the family mould and establish his own career: he dabbled in jobs as diverse as truck driving and newspaper publishing, while in his spare time in 1950 he began racing an ancient Bugatti, one of the many historic cars that could still be found in the Buenos Aires region.

Disillusioned with the Peron government, De Tomaso decided in 1955 to leave Argentina and establish himself as a racing driver in Italy; as a parting gesture, he drove his 2-litre Maserati in the 1000 Kilometres of Buenos Aires, taking second place in his class and coming seventh overall. He came back a year later to finish fourth and win his class.

In the meantime, he had entered the Maserati in the Florida 12-Hour Grand Prix of Endurance at Sebring, but retired after only 16 laps with a seized transmission; his co-driver, a tall blonde from Red Bank, New Jersey, named Elizabeth Haskell, with an established reputation for driving

small Siatas very fast, didn't get a turn at the wheel that day, but not long afterwards she married De Tomaso.

For 1957, De Tomaso linked up with the Maserati brothers and their Osca company; he and Isabelle (she changed her name) took the 1500 cc class in the Buenos Aires 1000 Kilometres, finishing sixth overall. Then, at Rouen, he won an 1100 cc race, defeating a team of Lotus cars, one driven by the marque's creator, Colin Chapman.

Over the next couple of seasons, De Tomaso enjoyed considerable success with Osca, including winning the Index of Performance at Le Mans in 1958, his co-driver Colin Davis, son of former Bentley Boy and journalist S. C. H. Davis.

But though the trend was for racing cars to go rear-engined, the Fratelli Maserati refused to break away from the front-engined design with which they had enjoyed such success.

So De Tomaso established his own company in late 1958 to build a rear-engined sports car with a 750 cc Osca power unit; completed the following year, this first De Tomaso car never raced because there was a dispute over the rights to use the engine, so De Tomaso continued racing with a conventional 750 cc Osca and a DB Panhard.

And in late 1959, he made his one and only appearance in a Formula One Grand Prix, driving a rear-engined Osca-powered car which retired after only 15 laps. That same year, he founded De Tomaso Automobili in Modena, starting by building racing cars often incorporating advanced construction methods, which seemed, however, to be deficient in proper development.

Determined to produce a road car, in 1963 De Tomaso designed a sheet steel backbone chassis, in which the Ford Cortina engine was accommodated at the rear, driving through a four-speed gearbox. The car had double wishbone independent suspension and disc brakes all round.

De Tomaso initially commissioned Fissore to build the coupé bodies for this chassis, which was christened the Vallelunga, but the deal turned sour, there was acrimonious litigation, 'We heard that De Tomaso couldn't go to Saviglione, where Fissore is located, because they were shooting at sight!' remembered a Ghia employee—and the job went to Ghia.

Filippo Sapino recalls that Segre had family links with Argentina, and feels that could be the reason why Ghia took on the De Tomaso contract despite Fissore's unhappy experience.

Unusually, while the prototype Vallelunga had been skinned in aluminium, the Ghia bodywork on production models was made of fibreglass, not beaten from the metal. De Tomaso claimed a top speed of 130 mph, and an early Vallelunga won the 1965 Italian Speed Championship.

Though a Ghia-built Vallelunga was chosen for a 1966 design exhibition in New York's Museum of Modern Art as 'an example of technological progress and outstanding design', those few who drove Vallelungas criticized the excessive vibration transmitted through the backbone chassis and the insufficient rigidity of the rear suspension, which was partly supported by the engine/gearbox unit. Total production of the Vallelunga was about 180 cars; deliveries to customers in Europe and America only really got under way at the beginning of 1967.

In 1965, Gaspardo Moro offered the job of head of the Ghia design studio,

LEFT The first car Ghia built for De Tomaso was the Vallelunga, a rear-engined Ford Cortina-powered sports coupé

BELOW The Barcelona showroom of Ibecar, who imported Ghia products into Spain in the 1960s, with examples of the Ghia 450/SS, 1500 and De Tomaso Vallelunga on display

which had been occupied by Coggiola, to a young stylist working at Bertone, Giorgio Giugiaro. For 'Giorgetto', it was a valuable stepping stone, the experience of working with companies such as Isuzu was a major contributory factor to his eventual decision to 'go it alone' with the formation of ItalDesign.

But Ghia hadn't finished with Exner, even though he had by now left Chrysler to go freelance. In March 1965 Exner bought the last Bugatti, a type 101C chassis which was one of six built for the 1951 Paris Salon. Five of them had been sold; number six—serial 10156—had languished at Molsheim for several years before being acquired by an American collector, who disposed of it to Scott Bailey, founder-editor of *Automobile Quarterly*. Scott kept it until the sale to Exner.

Exner, who had left Chrysler in 1961 to turn independent, was following a design theme that in automotive terms was akin to 'jazzing the classics'. In 1964, he had designed the gross 'Mercer Cobra' to show the decorative properties of copper and brass and revive the spirit of the handsome Edwardian Mercer Raceabout. With strange outrigged triangular wings and a dummy radiator shell that bore no resemblance to the original 1911 Mercer, the car was built on an AC Cobra chassis, though whether this was just an elaborate pun on the use of COpper and BRAss trim or whether it sprang from the suitability of the Cobra's tubular chassis for clothing with *jeux d'esprit* of this kind is unclear. The Mercer Cobra, though it was built in Turin, was the work of an obscure *carrozzeria*, Sibona e Basano; but when Exner came to choose a coachbuilder for that naked Bugatti chassis, he turned to his old collaborators, Ghia.

The Ghia Bugatti 101C was as odd, in its way, as the Mercer Cobra; it appeared at the November 1965 Turin Show and again proved how difficult it was to blend traditional radiators with modern full-width styling. Either side of the horse-shoe radiator were square headlamps nestling in deep recesses flanked by massive projecting wings. Virtually every panel was heavily louvred.

The rear-end treatment was much more successful, with neatly tapered rear wings, but the whole car had a curiously foreshortened appearance, the reason for which became clear when you read the press release: 'The original frame was shortened by 460 mm. . .'. That's 18 inches docked from a not excessively long chassis which looked at its best with two-seater bodywork, anyway.

Exner, who died in 1973, kept the car for some years, but used it very little and eventually sold it to Thomas Barrett III, a car collector from Scottsdale, California. Barrett disposed of the Ghia Bugatti to Irving Tushinsky, 'founder of Sony Superscope'. The car then went to a collector who wanted to remain anonymous, and is now in the San Diablo, California-based Blackhawk Collection owned by Ken Behring, a fabulously wealthy real estate developer. Yet after 20 years and five owners, the Ghia Bugatti still has less than 1000 miles on the odometer. If ever there was a car that was for show rather than go, this is sadly it.

Alongside the Bugatti on the Turin Show stand was the 5-litre Ghia-De Tomaso, representing the company's second commission from Alejandro De Tomaso.

Ghia's publicity promised that 'this is the car which is going to participate

ABOVE Anna, De Tomaso's personal assistant, with the Exner-designed Bugatti 101C, based on a bare chassis bought from Molsheim by an American collector and cut-and-shut by Exner to achieve that nose-heavy look

RIGHT The rear view of Exner's Bugatti is, perhaps, happier than the front . . .

in World Championship races under the name of Ghia . . . purity of line,
novelty in design and aerodynamic profile. A rear wing, with variable inclina-
tion, is mechanically controlled by the gearbox and helps to regulate the
pressure of the rear axle on the ground at high speed . . . the backbone chassis
incorporating engine and gearbox is an application of the principle introduced in 1962 by De Tomaso on a singleseat Indianapolis racer, a system
subsequently adopted in the construction of Formula One cars.'

'The very low centre of gravity and the solidity and rigidity of this new
chassis, keeping rolling to a minimum, give excellent handling and roadhold-
ing, allowing the driver to draw all the power from the motor to meet any
contingency.'

Perhaps the person most surprised at the car being exhibited as a Ghia-De
Tomaso was the American, Pete Brock, for he was the man who had actually
designed the aggressive aluminium bodywork round a backbone chassis built
by Piero Fantuzzi. The official explanation was that Ghia was financing the
car's racing programme, which, it was said, would begin with an entry in
the 1966 Sebring 12 Hours: but like so many of De Tomaso's sporting projects of the 1960s, nothing further came of it. . . .

A third prototype of 1965 to be launched at the Turin Show was a sports
two-seater on the 7-litre Cobra chassis; it was the result of a visit to Ghia
by Carroll Shelby, who knew De Tomaso from his racing days in America,
and who, along with Ford, had hired De Tomaso to develop a rear-engined
sports car that would supersede the Cobra. Shelby was accompanied by Ray
Geddes, who was Ford's link-man in the Cobra project. Geddes, who had
joined Ford as a financial analyst in 1961, met Carroll Shelby and became
involved in motorsport the following year. The idea behind the Ghia Cobra
was that this modern Italian-styled two-seater would replace the old AC

The AC-Ghia Cobra resulted from a trip to Ghia by Carroll Shelby and Ford link-man Ray Geddes, but this replacement for the old bluff-fronted Cobra body failed to pass the prototype stage

designed Cobra body, but in the event it was a similar, though not so stream-lined, body by Ghia graduate Pietro Frua which was chosen—by AC, not Shelby—to update the Cobra, though it was not a remarkable success, since the Cobra image relied more on brute strength than elegance.

Having lost the Cobra, De Tomaso decided to go one better, and Giugiaro was asked to create a new rear-engined sports car: it would be called *Mangusta*, Italian for 'mongoose'—the deadly enemy of the Cobra.

The chassis layout of the Mangusta followed what was becoming the tradi-tional De Tomaso plan: mid-engined, with a backbone frame. This time, the intention was for the chassis to be designed by Giotto Bizzarrini, already noted for the rear-engined GT Strada and Spider built under his own name, but he failed to deliver in time, and the prototype Mangusta was built round a chassis derived from the unsuccessful Brock/Fantuzzi-designed De Tomaso sports-racers of 1965. Giugiaro's silver-gold two-seater coupé body was the star of the 1966 Turin Show because of its classic simplicity; it stood just 43 in. tall, with huge gull-wing covers hinging on a dorsal rib giving access to engine, transmission, rear suspension and spare wheel.

Power was initially claimed to be by De Tomaso V8 of 4728 cc, but when the car eventually went into production in 1967, it was endowed with Ford's 5-litre V8. But if Ghia was becoming increasingly embroiled with De Tomaso, Virgil Exner still had one last card to play; it was revealed to a somewhat less than awestruck world in the spring of 1966 at a press reception held in the Sheraton-Lincoln Hotel in Indianapolis.

'Mighty Duesenberg reborn today!' trumpeted the headlines, announcing the launch of a modern 'four-door brougham sedan' bearing the name of what had once been America's finest car, produced in Indianapolis between 1920–37. But there was little attempt to copy the grandiose styling of the

ABOVE Designed by Giorgetto
Giugiaro, the Mangusta was
intended to be a Cobra-beater; in the
event, it looked better than it
performed

RIGHT Alejandro De Tomaso
demonstrating how low the
Mangusta is at the 1968 Turin Show

original Duesenberg in Exner's 1966 version: 'The new Duesenberg is completely modern in styling yet has touches reminiscent of its majestic forebears,' ran the 1966 press release, 'including the eagle emblem and the long, sleek hood. The hood is 82 inches long and the overall length of the world's longest production automobile is 20 feet 4.7 inches. Yet so well proportioned is the new Duesenberg that it represents a graceful flowing symmetry unique in automobile styling. The front fender styling has just a touch of the clamshell curves that marked the Duesenbergs of the 1930s.'

To say that the normal equipment of the Duesenberg was comprehensive was almost an understatement: 'The standard instrumentation includes an auto pilot, four season automatic climate control, a 20-decibel AM-FM radio, altimeter, speed indication up to 150 mph, odometer, tachometer, ammeter, plus water, temperature and fuel gauges. The Duesenberg has a 440 cubic inch V8 engine with 425 horsepower. Standard equipment includes full power disc braking on all four wheels, three-speed automatic transmission, adjustable steering wheel, six-position, electrically-operated front seat, chrome wire wheels and specially made 8.90/15 whitewall tyres.'

Equally, the Duesenberg was a car of superlatives: quite apart from its world-beating overall dimensions, it was said to have more head room, leg room and wider seats than any other production car, and more unobstructed boot space than any other standard American car.

The prototype was finished in magnum burgundy—'countless hours of hand rubbing and many, many coats of paint were necessary to achieve the deep, rich gloss'—with black vinyl roof, while the interior had cashmere upholstery and carpeting, with genuine mahogany panelling. However, noted Duesenberg president McMinis: 'Each Duesenberg sold will be finished to order, with the owner specifying his choices of woods, leathers, upholstery fabric and carpeting.' At a basic price of $19,500, the Duesenberg seemed quite a bargain. . . .

After the Indianapolis preview, McMinis and his minions set off for the land of the big buck, displaying the Duesenberg to invited guests at the Sagewood Country Club in Houston, Texas, and at the Statler Hilton in Dallas. It's been said in the past that production of the new Duesenberg began and ended with that magnum burgundy prototype, but Giacomo Gaspardo Moro corrected this opinion: 'The Duesenberg was built in a small series: the engine, which we knew well, was from Chrysler. I think we built around 50 cars.'

Around this time, too, Ghia was attempting to keep the Chrysler connection alive with the production of their own Chrysler-engined luxury car, the 450/SS, powered by the Chrysler Commander 273 4473 cc V8 engine, and available as a convertible with disappearing hood and concealed rear seats or as a hardtop; deliveries began in 1966, with the car priced at $12,000, and production continued far into 1968. Few, however, were sold.

A joint venture with America which was definitely restricted to the construction of only one car was the Thor of 1966–67, a Guigiaro-designed coupé on a front-wheel-drive Oldsmobile Toronado chassis. A handsome metallic blue two-seater coupé ('in which, however, thanks to the wide interior dimensions, even four persons may comfortably travel') the Thor was only marred by an excessively hunched rear wing line.

But the Thor was only one of a tremendous outpouring of new prototypes that Ghia constructed in 1966, most of them the work of the young Giugiaro. For De Tomaso there was the production version of the Mangusta and an open Cortina 1500-powered mid-engined two-seat sports car, the Pampero, derived from the Vallelunga and named for the fierce wind that sweeps across the pampas in De Tomaso's native Argentina. Independently suspended all round, the Pampero also had disc brakes on all wheels; it suffered from the same faults of vibration and poor suspension as the Vallelunga.

A 1966 prototype of stupendous insignificance was the curiously sexist 'Vanessa', promoted as the 'car for the woman'; this little hatchback was based on a Fiat 850 with Idromatic semi-automatic hydraulic transmission. Having assumed that the woman driver found difficulty in changing gear, the Vanessa also assumed that she couldn't read instruments, either, for instead of gauges, the car had a panel of warning lights and a speedometer that gave audible warning when the speed reached 50 and 100 km/h. Equally incomprehensible were 'the cigar lighter with warning bell and the fire-extinguisher which can also be used to inflate a punctured tyre'.

On the credit side, Vanessa incorporated a removable glass sunroof—one of the first appearances of this now universal accessory—electric windows and an ingenious top hinged loading hatch on the pavement side of the car.

But of far greater significance was a commission from Maserati for a two-seater coupé: the result was one of Giugiaro's masterpieces, the Maserati Ghibli, a classically sleek 280 km/h GT whose styling was widely admired and copied. The Ghibli went into production in 1967, with Ghia building three to four full-trimmed bodies daily on the little overhead dragline that could still be seen in the main hall of their plant until it was ripped out during renovation at the end of 1984.

The Ghibli contract could not, however, conceal the fact that Ghia was in financial difficulties: Leonidas Ramades Trujillo was tiring of his *divertissement* and anxious to sell. Alejandro de Tomaso, on the other hand, was seeking to extend his business; his brother-in-law was a director of Rowan Controller Industries, of Oceanport, New Jersey, and Isabelle de Tomaso convinced the Rowan board that Ghia would be a worthwhile acquisition. So, armed with Rowan finance, De Tomaso turned up at Ghia: not only did he acquire Trujillo's 75 per cent holding but also bought the Contessa Louise Segre's 25 per cent as well, she having given up hope that her two sons would move to Ghia.

'It was a real bargain,' Sapino recalls. 'There were quite a few unfinished cars included in the sale, and when De Tomaso had completed and sold these, in effect he had taken over Ghia for free!'

Once De Tomaso was in control, the purge started. Many people left, many were fired: those who remained co-operated to protect their jobs. Among those who left at this time were Filippo Sapino, who went to Pininfarina where, among other designs, he was largely responsible for creating the body for the flat-12 Ferrari 512, launched at Turin in 1971. Giacomo Gaspardo Moro left, too: 'With De Tomaso, I could do nothing. He was impossible!'

Whatever else they said about Alejandro de Tomaso, he certainly brought a sense of style to running Ghia. His office was a treasure house of antique statues and oil paintings; beside his desk was a brassbound barrel from Nel-

The revived Duesenberg built at Ghia was powered by a 7210 cc Chrysler engine; its comprehensively-equipped dashboard even included an auto-pilot

son's flagship *HMS Victory*. 'And then there were the Venetian plates,' recalls Bill Camplisson, who was a regular Ford visitor to the via Agostino de Montefeltro in De Tomaso's day. 'De Tomaso had a magnificent set of these antique plates, displayed on the walls. The story was that the plates came from his acting as official courier between the Italian Government and the British Museum when the two bodies wanted to exchange some valuable antique for another. De Tomaso would arrange the deal: his fee was another piece of lesser value.' And not only did De Tomaso also own a boutique on Rome's fashionable via Condotti, but the man who flew his private plane had once been Mussolini's personal pilot. . . .

With Rowan's finances—later in 1967, they also acquired an 80 per cent interest in De Tomaso Automobili and Ghia's facilities, De Tomaso immediately set about revitalizing the Mangusta for production. A new chassis was devised, with an arc-welded sheet steel backbone, which was largely fabricated by Ghia: the cockpit bulkheads, floorpan and central tunnel were all integral with the bodyshell, while a square-tube subassembly bolted to the back of the chassis carried the engine and transmission.

After the body/chassis of the Mangusta had been completed at Ghia, it was shipped to Modena where De Tomaso fitted the powertrain, using engines bought from Ford Industrial Products, initially a 289 cu. in. (4736 cc) V8 for Europe, the 302 cu. in. (4949 cc) V8 being adopted when the Mangusta was exported to America in 1969.

Production was slow to get under way, and few Mangustas were built during 1967. And once the cars began to get into the hands of their enthusiastic new owners, certain fundamental shortcomings began to make themselves obvious. The clutch was heavy, the air conditioning was of questionable efficiency, the windows wouldn't wind right down and the handling was treacherous, with low-geared steering allied to unpredictable rear-end breakaway. Add to that poor braking, lousy rear vision and an awkwardly offset driving position and you realize how much of the Mangusta's sales appeal rested on Giugiaro's brilliant styling.

In 1968, Ghia built a Mangusta Spyder, which, because of the separate chassis, was a logical and easily achieved step. Though Giugiaro had left Ghia the year before, he was still acting as consultant in a freelance capacity. Power was by the Ford 289 cu. in. V8, though De Tomaso billed it as a 'De Tomaso 8-V' (in fact, De Tomaso's sole contribution to the power unit had been the fitting of stronger valve springs and gas-flowing the ports in the cast-iron head). A five-speed ZF transmission and limited slip differential were fitted, and top speed was claimed to be 'more than 150 mph', which was almost certainly optimistic, since the closed Mangustas were rarely capable of exceeding 145 mph.

In a wondrously convoluted press release, Ghia claimed: 'After having obtained an undiscussed success with the coupé, Ghia now presents the roadster type of the Mangusta . . . the line of the new Mangusta has been studied in order to maintain the slimness necessary to its own sport characteristics . . . on the rear hood, lowered until the limit of encumbrance of the engine, there are two longitudinal series of slits that, besides making easier the hot air exhausting from the engine, have the aesthetic purpose of discontinuing the too wide smooth surface. . . .' Aesthetics, it seems, are what killed the awkward-looking Mangusta Spyder, on which the fixed side window frames

The Ghia 450/SS was a $12,000 series-production coupé or roadster with 4473 cc Chrysler V8 power: the show car is being loaded aboard a freighter at Turin Airport in 1966

were claimed to act as a roll cage: only one was built, and De Tomaso sold it to a foreign businessman.

Also shown during 1968 were a luxury limousine based on the Checker taxicab and the Maserati Simun. The Checker was a consultancy design by Giugiaro, intended as 'a high class car which is expected to compete on the US market with the most fantastic limousines . . . the body has been made with the search of a style absolutely new and, in the meantime, proportional and in affinity to the tradition of the most famous body-makers specialized in luxury sedan cars . . . the car is equipped with an air conditioner and, in order to avoid every annoyance to passengers, the air outlet has been placed in the bottom of the compartment'.

Compared with the standard Checker cab's no-nonsense 'brute force and ignorance' styling, the Giugiaro Checker was indeed a great improvement; but it appeared underwheeled for its size, while its roofline appeared to have

LEFT The 1967 Ghia Thor was a Giugiaro design on the 6965 cc front wheel driven Oldsmobile Toronado chassis

been designed round people wearing top hats: all in all, it hardly counts as one of Giorgetto's masterpieces!

And the Simun was a sports coupé designed as a complete contrast to the Ghibli, which ended up as a very similar project to the Vignale-built Maserati Indy; distinctive features were large side windows, a 'peculiar trapezoidal shape' for the tail and tail-lamp failure warning lights. Oh yes, and Ghia's fractured English specialist stressed in the press release: 'The upper line of the fender, very tighten in the hood and door side, has been interrupted by a relief which stresses the rear wheels presence: here it is, the old and traditional styling detail, that only by a right proportion can get interesting and new.'

Another luxury car built under the new management was the four-door Iso Fidia, 'glamorous and sober, large and luxurious, it joins a limited but evident sport mark to a new classicism'.

ABOVE The Pampero, shown at Geneva in March 1967, had all-round independent suspension, disc brakes and a mid-mounted 1498 cc Cortina engine

Ghia also built a sports coupé on one of the last Serenissimas in 1968: by that time Serenissima were only building the odd prototype (they closed down the following year), and the Ghia-bodied car had a 'herringbone' chassis with a mid-mounted 3470 cc V8 engine which gave it a top speed of 250 km/h (155 mph). 'In order to create something completely new,' claimed Ghia, 'the stylists have applied on the car an idea developed in the architecture field. That is, as the modern skyscrapers have the structure inside and the very light outside surface is hanged on the structure itself, so the Serenissima top structure is in the inside of the car (acting also as a roll-bar) and it is covered only by glass. In this way there are possibilities to create a light and slender line.'

Other unusual projects undertaken around this time included the 'Sno-Ghia', a half-tracked snow-scooter powered by a 297 cc Sachs engine—Ghia had designed the 'Bobby' moped for Sachs in the mid-1950s—and a GT 'Competition Fulvia 1600', which had large plexiglass side windows to save weight while racing and a remarkable extra feature. 'Like in a conjuring trick,' boasted Ghia, 'the body shape changes from a comfortable GT coupé into an aggressive and streamlined racing car. As a matter of fact, it is sufficient to push a button and from the rear side a mechanically orientable wing rises, which increases the rear wheel's grip in proportion to the increase of the speed. . . .'

There were also some electric city cars built for Rowan—the 1969 'Rowan' was claimed to have a range of 200 miles and be capable of running 60,000 km on a set of batteries, which were an entirely new type developed by Rowan Industries, who were working on a special fast charger capable of recharging the batteries in about 20 minutes, against the normal eight hours.

Two months after the final departure of Giugiaro, Tom Tjaarda returned as chief designer; he had resigned in 1961 after an argument with Segre, and designed Ghia's last Lancia. This was a classic two-door coupé called the 'Marica', Ghia claimed that this was 'a classic woman's name of Roman times', built on a shortened Flaminia chassis. Before long, however, Tjaarda was involved in a project that would prove far more crucial to Ghia.

Starting in June 1969, the Ghia styling section began a concentrated week's work which resulted in the construction of three fifth-scale models of a proposed new rear-engined Ford-powered sports car styled by Tjaarda. 'At that time, Mr Ford was still stinging from having his offer for Ferrari turned down,' says Bill Camplisson, 'and Lee Iacocca was egging him on to build a luxury Italian sports car.'

The Italian-born Christina Ford, Henry Ford II's second wife, had bought a Ghia-bodied Ghibli and fallen in love with the design; and Lee Iacocca, who was then president of Ford Motor Company, knew De Tomaso through Carroll Shelby. Both Christina Ford and Lee Iacocca, the son of Italian immigrants who had named him 'Lido' after the Adriatic resort where he was conceived, were enthusiastic over Italian high-performance cars. Both were convinced that Henry Ford's ambition of owing a prestige Italian sports car manufacturer, which had initially been frustated by Ferrari's rejection of Ford's takeover bid in the early 1960s, could be met within the De Tomaso organization.

So Ford men Ray Geddes and Larry Kasanowski were despatched to Ghia with instructions to turn the Mangusta into a 'Ford-Ferrari' which could

RIGHT Schematic diagram of Giugiaro's Fiat 850-based 'Vanessa' car for the woman driver, with such delights as 'Idromatic' transmission and 'Bombola Eolopress' . . .

BELOW Ghia's stand at the 1967 Turin Show, with examples of the Rowan city car, the De Tomaso Mangusta, the Maserati Ghibli and the Oldsmobile Thor, a remarkable exhibition of the talent of Giugiaro

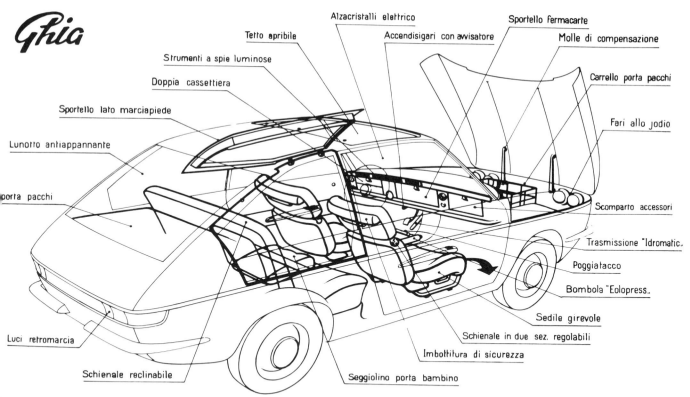

Ghia

Lunotto antiappannante

Sportello lato marciapiede

Doppia cassettiera

Strumenti a spie luminose

Tetto apribile

Alzacristalli elettrico

Accendisigari con avvisatore

Sportello fermacarte

Molle di compensazione

Carrello porta pacchi

Fari allo jodio

Scomparto accessori

Trasmissione "Idromatic"

Poggiatacco

Bombola "Eolopress"

Sedile girevole

Schienale in due sez. regolabili

Imbottitura di sicurezza

Seggiolino porta bambino

Schienale reclinabile

Luci retromarcia

porta pacchi

Vanessa

be sold in America through the Lincoln–Mercury dealer network at a price in the region of $10,000. They carried out a technical and quality assessment on the Mangusta: 'It was an absolute disaster, though the basic idea was good,' Bill Camplisson recalls. For many other reasons, the Ford Motor Company was not interested in getting involved with the Mangusta, even though the company had bought two Mangustas in 1968. But it was the designers, rather than the engineers, who had been captivated by the Mangusta, and the two cars ended up in the possession of vice president, Design, Gene Bordinat and his executive director, Don DeLaRossa, whose links with Ghia went back to 1952.

Prime reasons for the Ford engineers' rejection of the Mangusta were that the car failed conspicuously to meet most of the American Federal safety standards, and that its exemption from compliance with those standards expired in January 1970. But Geddes and Kasanowski found one of Tjaarda's models appealing, and recommended that it would be a good project for Ford to become involved with.

Lee Iacocca visited Ghia in August 1969: the welcome speech that De Tomaso made on that occasion now seems prophetic: 'I am sure that now, after the today's view, you will have a better idea of how we can work; however, first of all, I would like to do a remark: probably, because of our different mentality and working psychology and of our different dimensions, there will be many points, many working systems and even many decisions of ours that are incomprehensible from your point of view.

'Nevertheless I believe that the programme we are starting is very important and interesting: it can, no doubt, be very fruitful for Ford Motor Co,

At a Milan hotel in December 1968, Alejandro De Tomaso displays the new Ghia-bodied Maserati Simun, which has just won the _Gazzetta della Sport_'s coachbuilding award for Ghia SpA and for De Tomaso Automobili, SpA. The benefits will certainly arrive, provided that Ford Motor Co will realize that our greatest arm is the flexibility, the independence and the quickness with which we can work and decide. If this can be maintained, I can assure that the results will be excellent.

'Working against us are the factors of communication, confidence, comprehension and the opposition Mr Iacocca will find in his technical and style sections. These obstructions really exist and we must recognize them and be disposed to work towards a mutual comprehension about the different working and psychological conditions. If we are able to overcome these inconveniences with intelligence and diplomacy, I guarantee right now the success we will obtain.'

Ford obviously had the will to overcome these inconveniences, real or imagined, for on 9 September the company announced 'an agreement with Ghia Studios of Turin, Italy, and De Tomaso Automobili of Modena, Italy, for an exchange of technical services effective immediately. It is contemplated that Ghia/De Tomaso will build a number of Ford engineering prototypes, show cars and limited-build specialty vehicles.'

At the same time that the press release was being mailed, Ford designers were already in Turin giving their approval to a full-size fibreglass model of the Tjaarda design, and Ford had sent an engineer, a designer and a product planner on a one-year assignment with the De Tomaso organization.

Recalls Bill Camplisson: 'About that time, De Tomaso had fallen out with Maserati, and consequently promised if he dealt with Ford, he would stop making and trimming bodies for anyone else.'

'Filling a remarkable gap in the first-class cars market', the Iso Rivolta S4 (otherwise known as the 'Fidia') of 1967 was powered by a 5359 cc Chevrolet Corvette V8 engine

Production for Maserati was to continue for a little while longer, and when it ultimately ended, Ghia had built a total of 1274 Ghibli coupés and spyders: but the way was now clear for De Tomaso's planned cooperation with Ford. American journalists speculated that the proposed new Ford-powered car would be called 'Cobra II', but in fact it was destined for production under another name. An agreement was reached where the car, to be known as the 'Pantera', would be built at a planned rate of 5000 units a year and exported to the United States to be sold through selected Lincoln-Mercury dealers.

The task of solving the shortcomings of the Mangusta chassis was the responsibility of Ingegnere Gianpaolo Dallara, who had worked on the early stages of the Mangusta project before moving to Lamborghini to develop the Miura. De Tomaso had persuaded Dallara back to his fold with the bait of a promise that he could build a Formula One car.

Dallara replaced the whippy spine of the Mangusta with a monocoque chassis/body unit, whose main strength came from box-section sills that angled inwards at the rear to form the mounts for the engine and transmission. Power was by Ford's new 351 cu. in. (5752 cc) Cleveland V8 which was fitted as far back as possible, with forward-angled half-shafts: for increased ground clearance, the ZF transmission was mounted 'upside down' compared with the Mangusta, though equally this was the 'normal' position on the light trucks in which the ZF transmission was used in large quantities.

Ford of Europe was invited to cooperate in the Pantera project, and so Bill Camplisson was sent to Turin to meet Geddes and Kasanowski. 'Kasanowski was trying to use European bits in the Pantera,' says Camplisson. 'But when Ford of Europe was asked "Can you sell it in Europe?" the answer was a resounding "No!"'

Nevertheless, despite Ford of Europe's reluctance to get involved, Panteras were sold in small numbers in Europe by De Tomaso (who had retained the sales rights outside America) while the car was cleared by the US Federal authorities for sale in North America through the Lincoln-Mercury dealer network.

A prototype Pantera was exhibited at the January 1970 New York Motor Show, which closely resembled the production car: aerodynamic tests were subsequently carried out against a racing GT-40 and the 1970 Boss Mustang 302 in Ford's wind tunnel which proved that Tjaarda's design was efficient as well as elegant.

But, recalled Tjaarda when I interviewed him in Turin in 1984: 'The Pantera had gone from prototype to production in the extremely short time of eight months and there were inevitably teething troubles. The main one was the crash test carried out in California—the front wheels ended up under the driver's seat! They solved the problem by fitting a kind of double chassis.'

That disastrous crash test, the Pantera ultimately passed on the third attempt—must have been a deep embarrassment for the De Tomaso organization—for the official photographs are missing from the Ghia archives. . . .

Though the first few Panteras were built in the Ghia plant, the capacity there wasn't large enough to meet De Tomaso's future plans. Consequently, in December 1969, with Ford money now behind him, he acquired the Carrozzeria Vignale plant in Grugliasco (Turin). Vignale, despite its modern factory, located just behind the Fiat Mirafiori plant, was in financial diffi-

Not the aftermath of an accident, but a demonstration of how the 'very light outside surface' of a Ghia-bodied Serenissima sports-racer 'is hanged on the structure itself'. The giant hit-and-miss vents suggest problems with ventilation

culties. Since much of its income had been based on building special versions
of small mass-produced cars, which had universally gone over to unit body/
chassis construction, the production of special derivatives had become prohibitively expensive.

Alfredo Vignale, the master craftsman metal fabricator who had built up
the business he had founded in 1948 into a company with an international
reputation, took the loss of his *carrozzeria* hard; three days after the agreement transferring ownership had been signed, Vignale was dead, killed in
a crash in his Maserati. No-one else was involved; the car just ran into a
tree at night. To this day, no-one can determine whether it was an accident
or suicide. . . .

Nor were Vignale's death or the disastrous 50 km/h impact test the only
crashes to leave their mark on the company, for in New Jersey Rowan board
members Haskell and Ellis were attempting to land their light aeroplane in
thick fog when they flew into the ground and were killed. Immediately,
Alejandro de Tomaso arranged a personal meeting with Henry Ford II and
suggested a linkup between Ford and the De Tomaso group.

'The upshot was that one day in August 1970 we were at a meeting in
Warley with Bill Bourke, who was then president of Ford of Europe,' recalls
Bill Camplisson, now Ford-Britain's marketing director. 'He dismissed most
of the people in the room, and told us: "Mrs Ford has bought a Maserati
built by Ghia—and Mr Ford has now bought Ghia . . . so we need to get
involved."'

In fact, the Ford Motor Company had bought the 84 per cent of De
Tomaso shares held in North America by Rowan, the minority interest being

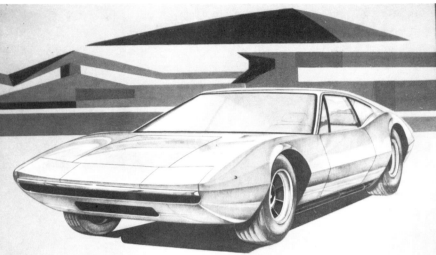

retained by Alejandro de Tomaso. As a result, a new holding company, De Tomaso (Delaware) Inc. was formed as an 84 per cent owned Ford subsidiary to operate as an autonomous, profit-centred organization within the Ford Motor Company. As president and chief executive officer of De Tomaso Inc, Alejandro de Tomaso reported to Ford's vice president of Product Planning. Ford finance man John D. Head was brought in to work with De Tomaso.

Coincidentally, Ford of Europe had founded its own Italian design studio, based at Bruino, near Turin, during 1970. Heading the staff of 20 working on advanced design concepts for the company's European range was ex-Ghia designer Filippo Sapino.

As mentioned above, while legal acceptance for the Pantera was being sought in America, the car was put on sale in Europe in small numbers during 1970. Some 285 'extremely uncivilized' Panteras were sold, mostly in Italy and England, even though the Vignale facilities were capable of building up to 16 cars a day.

Though the manufacture of Pantera had transferred to Vignale, all the production cars continued to carry the Ghia badge. Only two or three specially-built Panteras carried Vignale's badge, and those were built at Ghia!

Approval for US sales of the Pantera was finally granted in 1971; the Americanization of the car had not been without problems. Don Kopka re-

BELOW Rear view of the finished
Ghia Serenissima emphasises its
'light and slender line'

called a typical De Tomaso response during those early days when the Pantera programme was fraught with problems: 'De Tomaso came to Dearborn, where he had a morning meeting with the engineers, who complained that the Pantera's rear suspension didn't have enough clearance; "What do I know about that, I'm just an artist," replied De Tomaso.

'That afternoon, he met the design staff, who complained that the interior layout was seriously deficient. "What do I know of that, I'm only an engineer!" came the response!'

The task of sorting the Pantera for America was given to Ford troubleshooter Charlie Misenheimer, whose career had involved opening or reactivating Ford assembly plants in Argentina, Rhodesia, Brazil and Venezuela, as well as running the Dearborn pilot plant where advance models were assembled and tested.

Charlie's job of upgrading the Pantera's somewhat variable quality was aided by his chief test driver, the legendary Guerrino Bertocchi, who had helped build the first Maserati back in 1926 and sorted Fangio's 250F when the Argentinian driver won the world championship for Maserati in the 1950s.

While the Pantera saga was unfolding, Alejandro de Tomaso was developing an ambitious production programme in parallel, which he revealed to Ford of America executives in April 1971. It was aimed at scooping up a significant share of the worldwide 'fringe' markets, which he claimed consisted of six million vehicles, including sports cars, luxury cars, mini cars and recreational vehicles (in which he included motorcycles, snowmobiles and 'other types of motorized machinery').

The sports car segment (a claimed 7000 units) he saw as the province of the Pantera, which offered near-Ferrari levels of performance at less than half the price, plus a new Tjaarda-designed sports car, the Zonda, 'born of the collaboration between the styling centre of Carrozzeria Ghia and the styling centre of De Tomaso Automobili', and launched at the 1971 Geneva Show. Powered by a front-mounted 351 cu. in. Cleveland V8 with a De Tomaso overhead camshaft conversion, the Zonda was to be sold only in Europe, the intention being that it would not be federalized: production was planned for 500 units a year, and the car was intended to 'offer the prestige, performance and style of Ferrari and Maserati at a very competitive price' (between $12,000–15,000).

Also aimed at the sports car market was a proposed medium-priced model, the LMS, which had a light fabricated square-tube backbone carrying a four-cylinder twin overhead camshaft Ford BDA competition engine mounted transversely between the rear wheels, which it drove through a De Tomaso five-speed transaxle.

De Tomaso's plan was to offer the LMS with wedge-shaped 2+2 bodywork in 1973–74, with production planned at 6000 cars annually: in his opinion, the 12,000 sports cars of three types that he proposed to be selling in 1973 would 'establish a prestige image for Ford in the press, on the street and in the showroom to a degree far greater than that to be expected from the small number of units involved'. His intention was to 'pattern the company after the example of Porsche and build a company with an equivalent reputation, character and commercial success'.

A key factor in this plan was a new low-priced sports car code-named

Ghia's stand at the 1969 Turin Show with (left to right) the Maserati Ghibli Spyder, the 3 litre ohc V6 De Tomaso 2+2 and the Lancia Marcia

'Ancona', a Capri-sized hatchback sports coupé intended as a competitor for the Opel GT. Bill Camplisson was directly involved in this programme. He recalls that at the beginning of the 1970s the Ford Capri—'the car you've always promised yourself'—was riding high.

Ford policy is always to replace such a successful model at the peak of its popularity, so a team was established to develop a Mark II version of the Capri to be launched in 1974. Bill Camplisson was planning manager of that team: 'We decided to develop a hatchback, and one of our German designers, Hans Muth, really let his imagination roam. He came up with a really beautiful replacement Capri, it was all glass, tinted windows, frameless glass tailgate—and it was codenamed "Diana", after a secretary in Product Planning who was an inspiration to a lot of people involved in the project! The car was beautiful, with concealed lamps, and we recommended the Design Committee to try to go ahead with it.

'Henry Ford came to Europe and we showed him a mock-up Diana, a gold clay model that Lee Iacocca thought was fabulous. Mr Ford went over to look at the car, and the first thing he said was: "This ain't Capri!" The car had this elegant upswept window line, but Henry Ford traced an elliptical shape like the Mark I Capri window on the side of the car with his finger. "There," he said, "that's Capri . . . and by the way, I don't like the pop-up lights either!"

'Our beautiful creation had been rejected. Hans Muth left three months later to design motorbikes.'

Lee Iacocca subsequently told the team that while they had to concentrate on the design of a replacement Capri that was within the reach of Everyman, they should continue with the development of a car like the Diana—a prestigious low volume/high price speciality car.

'That was the start of Project Ancona,' Camplisson recalls. Ancona was to be an Italian-built car, based on either European Capri or North American Mustang powertrain and underbody. Iacocca had asked for estimates as to how many the US would take; on one of his earliest trips to Turin, Iacocca told Ghia: 'I'd like to see what you can come up with in the way of a nice little hatchback car in the best European tradition.' So Ghia began work on a project based on Hans Muth's original proposal, as a prestige import into the United States market.

Fifty-three days later they gave him the Ancona: it was a feat unheard of in Dearborn, where the span from drawing-board to prototype is measured in months rather than days.

Recalled Gene Bordinat, Ford's vice president, Design, at a press conference a couple of years later: 'Lee was astounded with the Ancona—and delighted. Here he was, sitting in the car, driving it, checking its seating, rolling down the window, putting his elbow out—all the things you do when you get a car "live". Ghia went a long way to proving its worth right there.

'But when it cames to quantity production,' Bill Camplisson told me, 'Ghia's facilities were hopelessly inadequate. De Tomaso's other recent acquisition, Vignale, couldn't handle the proposed quantity, either. So the search was on to find a company of the right capacity and offering the right quantity to handle the Ancona job.'

'A new project team was put together led by Leonard Crosland—now Sir Leonard Crosland—to find a body supplier, who could produce high-

De Tomaso's 'LMS' backbone chassis was intended for a medium-priced sports car; power was by a twin-cam 1599 cc Ford BDA engine

quality bodies-in-white to be shipped to Cologne for trimming and finishing. Crosland quickly identified Chausson in Paris, so in the early summer of 1970 we took the company's HS 125 executive jet to Le Bourget, and were whisked away to the Chausson factory in big Citroens.

'Chausson was run by the deputy Mayor of Paris, a highly-decorated, distinguished de Gaulle-like character named Abraham Chausson.

'So we were ushered into the office of this tall man with the ribbon of the Legion d'Honneur in his lapel, and Crosland asked him through the interpreter how much it would cost and so forth, then dropped his bomb-shell: "I want all the costings by September!"

"But," said Chausson, "nothing gets done in Paris in August—everyone's on holiday".

"I don't care," replied Crosland, "Ford Motor Company wants it done."

'Eventually Chausson conceded to all our requests and agreed that their complete engineering costing team would work through the summer holiday; they even paid the local Casino to stay open to feed everybody. Crosland appointed a three-man team—Malcolm Hendy, a British body engineer, Heinz Gulden from German manufacturing and a product planner, which was me—to spend August working with the Frenchmen.

'Anyway, they completed the job and presented their detail costings but in the meantime Iacocca had become disenchanted with the whole project, and was distinctly lacking in enthusiasm, based now on a more detailed business assessment. Even before we went to receive the official estimates, we had word from the States that Project Ancona was dead, but we went back to Chausson anyway, and there we were sitting in all that distinguished company. Crosland thanked them for a good job, and they replied that they had put in a lot of effort in the trust of big things coming.

'"Thank you very much," said Crosland, "but I'm afraid we don't want to go ahead."

'The big Frenchman just stood up and, followed by his entire board, walked out in absolute silence. It was left to the interpreter to dismiss our little group. We felt pretty low as we left clutching the nice personal note pads and gold-plated four-colour pens that had been presented to each of us earlier.'

Had Ancona gone ahead, Ghia's projections showed Chausson building 150 a day, 30,000 a year, representing a total investment of $13.3 million, with the possibility of increasing output to 300 cars a day to cover European demand in addition.

When the Ancona programme was dropped, De Tomaso came up with alternative proposals, one of which would involve Chausson supplying tools to DAF in Holland, who would then produce the entire vehicle, or for the entire project to be taken over by Karmann in Germany.

Though De Tomaso was hopeful that using these methods the Ghia Ancona could be revived for production in mid-1973, nothing came of the project. Nor did another Ghia-designed proposal for a new Mustang, Project Venice, based on three design studies carried out as part of the Ancona programme, survive the planning stage. The Venice was to have been available as a three-door coupé, two-door coupé and two-door Targa-top convertible, all of typical 'De Tomaso' appearance, but that programme never got off the drawing board.

More successful was Tjaarda's design for the Ghia luxury car, the Deauville, which had the 351 cu. in. V8 Ford engine with De Tomaso's overhead camshaft conversion in a lengthened version of the Zonda chassis. Though the company claimed that Italian *carrozzerie* rarely attempted to build four-door prestige saloons, and boasted that the Deauville 'reflected the tradition and the experience of famous Italian craftsmen', nevertheless the end product looked pretty much a carbon copy of the Jaguar XJ6!

The engineering standards of the Deauville did not impress Ford engineers: Bill Camplisson recalls a fast journey in an early car with Jack Hooven, vice president of Product Development, and Ralph Peters, vice president of Product Planning.

'We had just finished a meeting with Alejandro in his via Agostino de Montefeltro office when word came through that his pilot could not fly us out of Turin and on to Milan to pick up the company's 'plane because of rapidly closing fog.

'Acting in his incredibly decisive fashion, De Tomaso said: "You will leave now, with my best driver in my fastest four-seater and drive to Milan—and beat the fog!"

'We ran down to the courtyard and straight into a maroon Deauville—

RIGHT With a family resemblance to the De Tomaso 2+2, the Mustela was a 1970 Ford-powered prototype

BELOW Production in full swing at the Ghia plant with (foreground) De Tomaso Deauvilles and (behind) Maserati Ghiblis progressing down the drag line

which Jack Hooven initially thought was an XJ6. The driver was about 18 years old, about Tazio Nuvolari's size and had a close-cropped head with huge ears—I know, I sat behind him! With an imperious "Go quickly, my friends!" from Alejandro, we rocketed straight through Turin and on to the autostrada with lights blazing and frequent blasting from the air horns.

'What a driver! Jack, sitting next to me, was silent for the whole trip, but chain-smoked through a pack of Kents. His only other movements were to look over to the speedometer and put his hands flat against the rear floor transmission tunnel.

'Obviously, we made it, although I can remember the swirling leading edge of the fog literally following us along the autostrada and swallowing the Fiats in our 200-plus km/h wake! At the airport, Jack quietly got out of the car, knelt down and examined the rear suspension mounting points for a minute or so, then stood up and marched straight into the departure lounge. He didn't relax enough to describe his opinion of the Deauville's rear suspension engineering standards until his second Jack Daniels!'

Launched at the 1970 Turin Show, the Deauville without the twin-cam conversion began to reach customers in mid-1971, though whether output ever attained the intended 500–1000 units annually is a moot point.

In 1971, Ghia introduced the Longchamp, a 2 + 2 'elegant and aggressive coupé' derived from the Deauville. It was, suggested the company, 'the result of an accurate architectronic study and of calculations and aerodynamic tests'; once again, Tom Tjaarda was the designer, and the car was claimed to be capable of accelerating from 0–100 km/h in 5 seconds, despite the fact that 'the engine power is softly discharged by the torque converter and the general smooth engine operation'. The Longchamp went into production in 1972.

At the other end of the scale from luxury cars, De Tomaso proposed the building of a Ghia minicar to compete with the Fiat 500, the BLMC Mini, the Honda 600 or GM's proposed 'Sweet 16', which would have had a 56 in. wheelbase and Wankel rotary engine had it seen the light of day.

Ghia had begun work on two hatchback city car prototypes in 1970, one built on a Fiat 500 platform, the other a stubby three-seater built on a 13 in. shorter wheelbase than the Fiat 500 and powered by a 500 cc Steyr-Puch flat-twin. It was a remarkable two feet shorter overall than the first De Tomaso city car, and looked as though it had been involved in a traffic shunt!

Finally, there were the recreational vehicles, and here De Tomaso trotted out some Ghia design studies for all-terrain vehicles, the Sno-Ghia, motor-cycles (he already owned two of Italy's biggest motorcycle manufacturers, Benelli and Moto Guzzi) and Project Como. Como was to be a 'multi-application vehicle' powered by a De Tomaso 1000 cc air-cooled power pack with integral suspension attachment driving the rear wheels, though front-wheel drive was being studied. Among the myriad applications considered for Como were pick-up, van, bus, camper, dune buggy, off-road and in-plant haulage. . . .

The proposed expansion of the activities of the De Tomaso group 'to face all those market opportunities which are too small for Ford' was quite unrealistic, considering the plant at its disposal, and that the group wasn't even halfway to meeting the original targets for the Pantera; nor was the Deauville

LEFT Detroit shows its hand—Don DeLaRossa's 'interpretation' of a Ghia design became the Mustang II

BELOW De Tomaso's reworking of the 1972 Ford Granada met with a less than enthusiastic response from Ford of Europe

a runaway success. During 1971, Pantera sales in America were only 130: in 1972 they reached 1552.

Those early Panteras were notorious for overheating; one of the Ford team working in Turin at the time recalled a 1973 conversation with De Tomaso while they were working on a prototype Pantera for 1975.

'"You really ought to do something about that overheating problem," said a Ford engineer. De Tomaso's reply was typical: "Just put a 5 ohm resistor in the line between the temperature sender and the gauge!" That certainly made the gauge reading lower, even if it didn't actually cure the overheating!'

De Tomaso also attempted to interest Ford of Europe in other projects, at the recommendation of Lee Iacocca, who, Bill Camplisson recalls, said: 'Ghia is a great design and custom house—why can't we use their services as a "designer label" for European Fords?'

So De Tomaso built a few Mustang-engined concept cars and shipped them to Ford's Design Centre at Dunton, Essex. 'The European directors,' Camplisson recalls, 'told De Tomaso, "These aren't the sort of cars we want for Europe!" And their technical head, vice president Jack Hooven, went even further, and said that he thought their engineering standards were "abysmal". . . .'

'So Bill Bourke said: "Why don't we take on things we can bite off, and ask De Tomaso to customize the new Granada?"'

De Tomaso's first attempt was a mildly customized Granada with airvents in the wheelarches, grained leather upholstery and a new taillight housing. Cheekily, he badged the car as a 'De Tomaso'; the only clue to its actual builder was a tiny 'powered by Ford' notice on the boot lid. Then De Tomaso set about building something far more grandiose, in keeping with the American concept of what a luxury car should look like.

'When we were told that the De Tomaso Granada was ready,' Bill Camplisson told me, 'I went over to Ghia with designer John Fallis, to look at the car. We cringed. . . . The car was brought over to Dunton. Everybody cringed again. . . .'

Revised rear end styling of the 'De Tomaso' Granada—the tiny 'powered by Ford' badge raised corporate hackles

'So Bourke called Iacocca and told him nobody liked what De Tomaso had done to the car—I remember it had the spare wheel shaped in the boot lid like the Lincoln Continental—but Iacocca said it was just a case of Not Invented Here. So Bill Bourke asked De Tomaso to pull in the reins and have another go. In the meantime, the decision was taken to have the car, which was called the "Ghia Mark I", market researched at the 1973 Geneva Salon to gauge public opinion.'

Moreover, the Ghia studios were also getting involved in the creation of prototypes for future Ford models. In the autumn of 1972, Don DeLaRossa, who acted as link man between Ford's Dearborn Design Centre and Ghia, was asked to order a styling study from Ghia for the new 'Project Bobcat' mini car programme. Recalled Tom Tjaarda when I met him in the autumn of 1984: 'The task of designing the Bobcat was dumped right in my lap. And what was remarkable about the whole project was that from drawing board to running prototype took just 56 days. I remember that Lee Iacocca was very impressed!'

Built on a Fiat 127 platform, the 'Blue Car' was the most attractive of all the prototypes developed in Ford styling studios on both sides of the Atlantic; Tjaarda refined its design into the 'Wolf', a little yellow coupé which formed the basis of the final design of the Bobcat, which was launched in late 1976 as the Fiesta, perhaps the most significant new car Ford had introduced since Model T, for it not only marked Ford's breakthrough into the mini car field, but also saw the building of an entirely new plant in Spain. It represented an investment of a billion dollars.

But though Ghia was now proving a valuable asset to Ford, Alejandro de Tomaso was about to drop his bombshell. Only a year before he had boasted: 'We are proud to say that we work for Ford and are part of the family of Ford people.' Now he announced: 'Because of my expanding industrial and commercial interests in Italy other than Ford, I evaluated the need to devote an increasingly major part of my time to these interests. They include two of the largest motorcycle firms in Europe, of which I am president: F.lli Benelli SpA and SIEMM Moto Guzzi, both of Italy. In view of these responsibilities, I initiated conversations with Ford, which resulted in my decision to resign as president of De Tomaso Inc., and from Ford Motor Company.'

On 8 January 1973, Ford announced that it had bought Alejandro de Tomaso's 16 per cent minority holding, and that De Tomaso Inc. would immediately be renamed 'Ghia Operations'. But Alejandro de Tomaso retained one crucial link with the new Ghia organization: after discussions with Ford, he announced that he had become Pantera distributor for Europe.

He also retained his personal links with Lee Iacocca after the break with Ford; in the early 1980s, after Iacocca's stormy departure from Ford and his spectacular revival of Chrysler (where Don DeLaRossa joined him as head of design after retirement from Ford), De Tomaso signed an agreement with the Chrysler Corporation to build new prototypes for them. Drawings of a somewhat exaggerated 'Chrysler-Maserati' two-seater sports car were published early in 1985. One clause of the contract gave Chrysler the right to use the name 'Pantera' in the future. . . .

5 Ford takes control

Visitors to Ghia after it had come under full Ford control would have noticed one immediate difference on entering Jack Head's office: gone were the antiques, the Venetian plates and Nelson's barrel; in their place was 'a unique gallery of styling studies of how cars at present produced in Ford's American, European, Asia-Pacific and Latin-American plants may develop in the coming decades'.

Another result of the change of control was that the Italian Design Studio which worked for Ford in Europe at Bruino, near Turin, was merged with Ghia during February 1973. The chief designer at Bruino, who now became chief designer at Ghia, was Filippo Sapino, who had started his career 11 years earlier at Ghia in the days of Gigi Segre.

Though he had no formal art training, Filippo's drawings and ideas had been of such quality that Segre had invited him to join Ghia at the age of 20. It was his family background which had kindled Filippo's interest in cars: 'I have loved them since I was two years old—even though my family could never afford one. The fact that my father worked in a local car factory might have had something to do with it, but I do not really know why—you will have to ask Freud. I only know that I have always drawn cars—as long as I can remember. I was always being caught by the teacher drawing cars when I should have been doing mathematics. . . .'

Another factor in Filippo's passion for cars was that, while the family could never afford a car when he was a child, his father did race a Dollar motorcycle, a well-known French sporting make whose posters depicted a Red Indian at speed on a Dollar 'bike.

Between his first seven-year stint at Ghia and joining the Bruino Design Studio, Filippo Sapino had spent a couple of years with Pininfarina working on both interiors and exteriors, as well as creating that sensational body for the flat 12 Ferrari 512.

The first car to be shown publicly bearing the names of Ford and Ghia was, perhaps, not the happiest choice, for it was that 'orphan' Ghia Mark I, De Tomaso's luxury version of the Granada. What had been attempted was to transform the Granada into a miniature Rolls-Royce by grafting on the radiator of a Lincoln Mk IV and quadruple headlamp installation, as well as American-style bumpers and a boot lid with a simulated spare wheel housing.

RIGHT ABOVE The first fruit of the Ford-Ghia union was the Ghia Mark I, an attempt to turn the Granada into a little Rolls-Royce

RIGHT Mustela II was a more aggressive interpretation of the 'Mustela' concept; again, it had 3 litre Ford power

136

Jack Head, who had been handed the 'Mark' programme as his first objective as president of the new group, put on a brave face: 'We have consciously developed Ghia operations to become a major new force supporting Ford in Europe. With the Mark I—our first product to be publicly exhibited on a Ford stand—we have aimed for the quiet, smooth and comfortable Granada ride allied to the highest standards of Italian craftsmanship. The interior is exclusively a Ghia approach, and I think that this model may well have a place in the future.'

Some 200 visitors to the Ford stand at Geneva were handed a 'self-completion questionnaire', on which they were asked to note their options of the front, side, rear and overall exterior views of the Mark I, its interior comfort and appearance, things they liked and disliked about it, their 'projected images' of the car, what they thought it would cost and an overall evaluation of the project.

'The general response was that the Mark I was an "abortion"!' recalls Bill Camplisson. 'But the ultimate version of the car was far more tasteful, and became the first Granada Ghia. During the spring and summer of 1973, everyone warmed to the design, which was passed to the manufacturing division to investigate the feasibility of producing the car in series.

'But then we hit a real problem. Volkswagen complained bitterly to the Italian Government that the right to use the name Ghia on a series production car was exclusively theirs on the Karmann Ghia, and it would be wrong to use the name Ghia on a Ford.'

After a frantic round of talks between Ford of Europe president Bill

ABOVE Piloted by Tom Tjaarda, this was a 1973 Ghia design study for a Ford Urban car

RIGHT Quart into pint pot department: this rear-facing foldaway third seat was featured on a 1973 small car study, the Ghia Mini Max

Bourke, the Italian Government, Volkswagen and Ford US, it was finally agreed that the Ghia studios were genuinely producing designs for the top range of European Fords, and that Ford was fully entitled to use the Ghia badge on its products.

Jack Head defined the new role of Ghia within the Ford organization: 'Ford's Advanced Vehicle Operations have successfully offered performance versions of standard production cars. I hope that Ghia Operations can provide the same formula, but in a different direction—by providing first class design treatment. Obviously we shall not abandon our traditional role of designing and executing exciting cars like the Pantera and Mangusta— projects of this nature are currently in process in our design studios.'

Filippo Sapino recalls that shortly after the Ford takeover of Ghia, he received a visit from a man representing a group of Brazilian millionaires. They, apparently, all owned identical Rolls-Royces, and wanted Ghia to customize each one. 'But I had to tell him we could no longer do such work now we were owned by Ford.'

The first performance model from Ghia Operations was, in fact, shown on Ghia's stand at the 1973 Geneva Show: called the Mustela II, it was a revised version of a Tjaarda design shown at Geneva three years earlier. Designed around the Ford 3 litre V6 Essex engine, the Mustela II was intended as a preview of some of the design ideas that would be incorporated in the 1974 Capri II, like the rear hatch and the new alloy wheels; it also incorporated an experimental turbocharger installation which boosted the power output of the Essex engine to 180 bhp.

Meanwhile, that abortive project Ancona was having an effect on the shape

of American Fords to come. Though the design hadn't been adopted for the European Capri II, it had been used as a concept car for the proposed 1974 Mustang II. Said Iacocca: 'It coalesced the different opinions of people in a hurry.'

The upshot was that Ford's Dearborn Design Centre ran a design contest among four of its own studios, based on the 'package' of the Ancona, which was won by a team of young designers from Lincoln–Mercury. But the project was continually changing, and in May 1971, it was decided that Mustang II should be smaller, 'since the market for smaller cars was booming'. While Dearborn was rethinking its designs, a prototype was commissioned from Ghia.

'Our car from Ghia turned out to be very different from what we were working on in Dearborn,' said Gene Bordinat. 'For one thing, it had a concave roof. But more importantly, it was sculptured, more classically European.

'Mr DeLaRossa was very impressed by the basic design of the car under construction. And when he got back to the States after one of his visits to Turin, he began a variation of that Ghia prototype. He completed his car in August 1971. The Ghia car, made in metal, arrived in September. Both were shown to our Design Committee that month. The domestic version of the Ghia car won a tentative acceptance, with provisos for certain front-end modifications that made it conform more closely to the progenitor from overseas.'

So Mustang II, launched in September 1973, and the first Ford production model to carry the Ghia badge, was, in effect, a committee design job: nor was the end result a happy one.

Quoted Bordinat: 'It's as American as apple pie and pizzazz, as Italian as pizzazz without the final z's. . . .'

Doug Blain of *Car* was more forthright: he just called the Mustang II 'unspeakably ugly'!

Europe fared a great deal better with its first Ghia-badged car, the Granada

ABOVE Another Ghia redesign of the Taunus/Cortina, this time a saloon instead of a fastback

LEFT ABOVE By 1973, Ghia was fully involved with mainstream Ford projects: this is a proposed facelift for the Mark III Taunus/Cortina

LEFT BELOW Front view of the 1973 Ghia proposal for the Taunus/Cortina saloon

Ghia, launched on 16 January, 1974, which had a distinctive die-cast grille and headlamp surrounds, as well as Ghia-designed interior trim.

Said Bill Bourke, who had now been promoted to chairman, Ford of Europe: 'It's when you really get down to the detail that you can see why the Granada Ghia is such a powerful challenge to the best of the specialty luxury cars built by our European competitors. It proves that luxury, reliability and practical motoring can be achieved in the same motor car at a sensible price.'

You'll remember that 1974 was not a good year for motoring; but amidst all the misery of that first traumatic energy shock, Ghia brought out an extrovert showcar called the 'Coins', intended to show what the Capri might look at towards the end of the century. It was shown at the 1974 Geneva Salon, and, said the Ghia publicity, 'combined aerospace technology with advanced auto safety features'. This, it was claimed, would result in a car that was only half the weight of a normal Capri and had a very low drag factor, so that it could exceed 70 mph with an engine developing a mere 40 bhp.

'The objective,' claimed Ford, 'was to style a car which proved that even in a world where fuel shortages and speed restrictions limited driving, a sporty and exciting car could be conceived for those who like motoring for fun.'

But though the name Coins was inspired by the Roman habit of throwing coins in the Trevi Fountain for luck, no amount of wishing could make anyone believe that the keenest motorist of the 1990s would fall for a wedge-shaped three-abreast car where the driver sat in the middle and the only means of entry was by clambering through the hatchback and over the seats. Not even Tom Tjaarda, who designed Coins, remembers it with affection!

If Coins was not a universal success, behind the scenes Ghia was well in touch with reality; during 1974 the studios turned out 17 different design studies for forthcoming Fords, despite the encircling gloom of the energy crisis—in 1970, it had built just four prototypes. . . .

But that energy crisis didn't leave Ghia Operations unscathed. In the first nine months of 1974, factory sales of the Pantera only reached a total of 712 cars. The heady days of 1973, when the early teething troubles of the Pantera had been overcome, when 2033 Panteras were sold and a special 'Pink Pantera' was built for *Playboy* magazine's 'Playmate of the Year', seemed a lifetime ago.

In Europe, the nine-month sales of Pantera had collapsed by over 80 per cent, from 508 in 1973 to just 78 cars. Moreover, California had just promulgated strict emissions standards, requiring a significantly lowered percentage of nitrogen oxide in the exhaust gases, which effectively barred this profitable market to the Pantera: these requirements would become even stricter for 1975.

The cost of redesigning Pantera to meet the California emissions standards, considering the small production volumes involved, would have been prohibitively expensive, and technically tricky. The re-engineering of the front end of the Pantera to provide 5 mph impact-proof bumpers had been within the capability of the Ghia craftsmen: the new requirements would have piled yet another load on Ford engineers faced with a myriad tasks thrown up by the oil crisis. Moreover, the demise of the luxury car market

Watched by designer Tom Tjaarda, Pietro Brovarone, the manager of the Ghia plaster shop, works on the bootlid of a 1973 concept car

143

LEFT ABOVE Most famous product of the collaboration between Ford and De Tomaso was the Pantera, launched in 1968 and still in limited production at De Tomaso's Modena plant today

LEFT BELOW Ghia's Tuareg concept car based on the Fiesta attracted so much attention that Germany's Schwaben Garages built this 'production' version in 1978

ABOVE Filippo Sapino's futuristic 'off-road' concept recreational vehicle, the 'Montana Lobo', dates from 1979

was proving expensive: every Pantera sold represented a loss of several thousand dollars, and some dealers were reported to be unloading the $10,000-plus Panteras at $7000 just to stay in business.

On 24 October, Jack Head announced in Turin that Vignale, which was losing several million dollars annually, was to discontinue production of the Pantera and close the Grugliasco plant on 30 November, 1974. There were about 550 unsold Panteras left in American dealerships, and once those had been unloaded, new Pantera sales in the US had ended. But De Tomaso, who still had sales rights outside the United States, acquired the hundred-odd unfinished cars that were still in the Vignale plant, and resumed production on a limited basis in the De Tomaso plant at Modena, where Panteras are still being produced.

It had, perhaps, been expecting too much for a traditional *carrozzeria* to build and market a 160 mph supercar with all the production engineering that involved; in any case, the slimmed down Ghia Operations was fully occupied with its work on forward car programmes for Ford, with no fewer than 23 prototypes constructed during 1975, almost as many during 1976.

In the latter year, Tom Tjaarda left Ghia to join Pininfarina; since then, he has worked at the Fiat Design Centre (established in the late 1950s by Felice Mario Boano and his son) and at Rayton Fissore, where he designed the Saab Viking. His new Dimensione Design Company works on a wide range of projects: 'I studied architecture at university, and I still design homes and boutiques as well as cars.'

Ghia produced a remarkable show car in 1977, the Megastar, a swoopy four-seater with tinted side windows cutting deep into the doors. Eyecatching as this car was, it very nearly didn't survive its first outing: 'We took the car out to take the photographs for the press release,' recalls Ford's chief

ABOVE This 1979 'international car of the future', the Ghia Navarre, was a slightly uneasy joint venture between Ghia and the Dearborn Design Centre

OPPOSITE Shown side-by-side on the Ghia stand at the 1979 Geneva Salon were the 'longest and shortest Ford Fiestas', the GTK (foreground) built on an extended Fiesta floorplan and the Microsport energy conservation project

photographer Ken Shipton. 'Filippo was driving, and all went well until he had to stop. When he applied the pedal, there was just a scraping sound, and it took ages to bring the car to a halt. Megastar was built on a Granada chassis, which had been in the Ghia store for some time. The plant mechanic had "borrowed" the disc pads from the chassis intended for Megastar when the Ghia company Granada needed its brakes overhauled. . . .' A second Megastar appeared the following year: this time, a Taunus chassis was used, though the styling was much the same.

Built on the Fiesta chassis were the Corrida, an angular sports coupé introduced at the 1976 Turin Show which had a long, droop-snoot front plus gull-wing doors, and the Tuareg, shown at Geneva in 1978. The latter, a concept for a small off-road vehicle, caused so much interest that Germany's largest Ford dealer, Schwaben Garages of Stuttgart, offered replicas for sale, which it constructed round standard production Fiestas, working entirely from photographs of the Tuareg.

Another Fiesta-based concept car, the Microsport, first appeared at the 1978 Turin Show: 'it was', said Ford, 'a super-lightweight energy conservation project', which was 10 in. shorter and 10 per cent lighter than the standard Fiesta, thanks to the use of aluminium body panels, plus lightweight

The dashboard of the Ghia GTK had an elaborate liquid crystal display controlled by an on-board computer

instrument console, seat frames and upholstery.

The year 1978 also saw Filippo Sapino's 'Action' design study for a competition car intended to be powered by a rear-mounted DFV Formula One V8 3-litre engine; the novel feature of the Action's design was the front spoiler, whose line was followed along the side of the car to form a wide skirt completely enclosing the rear wheels.

The following year, Ghia built an odd sport coupé called the Navarre, which had been conceived by the Dearborn Design Centre to 'combine European design themes with the latest down-sized US vehicle dimensions'. A sporting five-seater coupé, it was designed as a multi-purpose car, with a load-carrying platform mounted on the boot lid, which was neatly merged with a concave rear window. The roof and boot lid were covered in tan vinyl 'to convey the impression of a convertible top . . . embryonic "sails" at each side form streamline fences to contain the flat area of the deck lid'. Mercifully, the Navarre was not widely exhibited after its debut at the April 1979 New York Show.

Far more typical of what Ghia could do was the Fiesta GTK, which was, said Filippo Sapino, 'a logical development of the Megastar concept.' Aimed at providing maximum interior accommodation within a package very little

The GTK's three-door estate body was designed, it was claimed, to create 'ground effect' for improved handling

larger than that of the normal production Fiesta, the GTK was based on an 1117 cc Fiesta Sport floorpan stretched by 4 in. Its three-door estate car body was designed to create 'ground effect' for improved handling, and the spare wheel was housed in the low, aerodynamic nose directly above the transmission. A futuristic touch was the on-board computer and liquid crystal instrumentation, housed in a module in front of the driver. Once again, Ghia was acting as a sounding board for concepts that could find their place in future Ford products.

Another futuristic flight of fancy from 1979 was an exciting aerodynamic two-seater based on the Ford Mustang, which was unveiled at the Frankfurt Motor Show in September. Called the RSX (for 'Rallye Sport Experimental'), the Ghia car was lower, shorter, narrower and lighter than the standard four-seater Mustang; a dramatic feature was a dished aerodynamic spoiler moulded from laminated glass as an integral part of the rear screen and tailgate.

RSX appeared to have doors made entirely of glass; the effect was achieved by bonding black tinted plexiglass panels to the lower door panels, which were side impact absorbent. Fixed side windows were used, since the RSX had a full air conditioning and ventilation system, though small hinged side panels were incorporated in each side window so that the occupants of the car could pay motorway tolls or talk to people outside.

Filippo Sapino, who had taken over from Jack Head as vice president of Ghia in 1976, voiced a standard Ghia design philosophy in describing the car: 'Although the Mustang RSX is a design which is directed principally towards fuel conservation, a most important part of our brief was to retain Mustang's traditional personal and sporting appeal so that it remains a vehicle which is still fun to drive.'

This sports car design study of 1979 was the Ghia Mustang RSX; the rear spoiler was moulded as part of the glass tailgate

6 Ghia in the eighties

So where and how does Ghia fit into the Ford organization in the 1980s? Obviously the Ghia badge is a familiar sight on the top of the range Fords, but that is just a sign of design input, for it would be impracticable and costly to build all the Ford Ghia models in that little plant in Turin, just as it was impossible to build the Karmann Ghia there—Ghia just isn't capable of large-scale production.

So in that case the Ghia badge just denotes the *carrozzeria*'s involvement at the early design stages of a programme, the submission of interior trim strategies for future models.

But what of the unique skills of Ghia? Where do they fit in to the complex world of Ford? I asked Uwe Bahnsen, Ford of Europe's vice president, Design: 'Because Ghia is so deeply involved in forward model programmes, many of the cars it builds can never be shown publicly. To some extent, that deprives Ghia of the public visibility it needs to strengthen its reputation as a coachbuilder. However, under Don Kopka, Ghia is moving in the right direction, as he is encouraging Ghia to be international where in the past it's been biased towards North American programmes.

A Ghia craftsman begins to form a steel panel with a power hammer

'As a research studio, it can realize truly innovative design concepts that are less closely linked with forward programmes. Equally, it can build show cars that can help to communicate a new concept philosophy to the world.

'I'd like to see Ghia given even greater independence to produce creative new vehicle concepts, because Ghia can draw on the quite exceptional skills that exist uniquely in Piedmont. That region is second to none in the way that apparently ordinary metal beaters have a finely developed sense of perception of form and surface values that results in a design concept being enhanced by their interpretation.

'Ghia's trade mark is elegance and that gives us the unbelievable opportunity of the Ghia craftsmen to shape our volume-production vehicles. Ghia's flair for elegance is echoed in the top of the line variants of Ford products—hence they carry the Ghia badge.'

In recent months, the Dearborn Centre has begun sending promising young designers to Ghia on short term assignment, allowing their talents to develop in a creative atmosphere from the peculiar pressures of forward model programmes. It's a trend that could develop fruitfully in years to come.

But what is it that gives Ghia its particular design ability? Filippo Sapino

believes that it's something unique to Turin: 'The natives of Turin have special characteristics among Italians—they are the country's artists and technicians, that's why they make such good car designers and manufacturers. Turin has always been first to take up all branches of technological innovation; you'll find that Turin was the leader in cinema, television, radio, electricity, computers. . . . I think that the people of Turin are rather like the Japanese: they're very productive, but also very stubborn, and creative in taking up new ideas. If you want commercial skills, you go to Milan, and for bureaucracy it's Rome. But for technology and engineering you must come to Turin!'

Not only that, adds Filippo, but the area also breeds metalworkers of outstanding ability, whose skills have evolved over generations, starting with those independently-minded *calderai* whose craftsmanship was devoted to the creation of ornamental brass and copperware.

There has been a decrease in their numbers over recent years due to the onward march of mass-production—it was easier for a metalworker to earn a good wage working in a car factory than at his craft—but the status and pay of skilled metalworkers has improved radically in recent years. Turin has now instituted a training programme for young men to learn the craft and keep the city's unique worldwide reputation alive and flourishing.

Today, Ghia is perhaps the last of the traditional *carrozzerie* in central Turin, and can turn out anything up to 23 prototypes a year, made up of drivable cars and static models, the latter mostly made from a special wood/resin compound called Epowood.

'Our staff today numbers about 80 people,' says Sapino. 'They consist of five or six designers, 25 workers in the metal shop, 12 modellers, 12 people involved in paint and trim, six engineers and the rest are involved in our administrative and other office work.'

Ghia is a unique repository of craft skills, and one of the last places where cars are still made in the traditional way of the old *carrozzerie*. After the designers have drawn up a series of concepts for a new Ghia prototype, full-scale drawings of the chosen model are made from which the woodworkers build an accurate 'hammer form', a wooden skeleton which the panelbeaters

OPPOSITE Forming a wheelarch over an anvil, using skills that have been handed down since the days of the *calderai*

LEFT Working on one of the complex sub-assemblies that go to make up a Ghia concept vehicle

use as a reference in the shaping and fitting of panels. The framework of the body is built up in square- or round-section metal tubing, to which the panels are attached.

Nowadays, because the wooden form is really unnecessarily robust for one-off prototype work—panels for up to 200 cars can be taken off such a form—Ghia is tending to use composite wood/plaster models which can only be used once. Either way, the quality of the finished bodywork is impeccable: no wonder other car companies openly envy Ford's Torinese think tank!

There's no easier way of proving the unique nature of Ghia than actually driving the product: and at Ghia the first test run of a new prototype is achieved with such studied nonchalance that you might just be taking the family car for a drive instead of a prototype worth several hundred thousand dollars, as I found when I first visited Ghia in the spring of 1982 to prepare the press release on the Brezza. This was a concept for an aerodynamic sports car that was to be the Ghia showpiece at that April's Turin Salon. . . .

It was a beautiful clear spring morning as the British Airways Trident crossed Lake Geneva and over the Alps; then, as we flew over the southern Alps, long fingers of mist began trailing from the peaks, merging into an impenetrable white fog that blanketed Piedmont from view. Turin Airport, an announcement told us, was closed, as it so often is when fog descends on the Po valley: we would have to land at Genoa, on that perilous-looking runway that sticks out into the harbour beyond the shipyards.

Nearly four hours late, after an interminable coach journey along the *autostrada* that threads through the mountains from Genoa to Turin, and having discovered that the Torinese taxi driver who knows how to find the via Agostino de Montefeltro is a rare breed, I ultimately arrived at Ghia to meet Filippo Sapino and see the new Brezza.

Downstairs in the long arched workshop where Ghia used to build bodies

RIGHT ABOVE Photographed by the elaborate fountain in Turin's Valentino Park, the Avant Garde was an attractive coupé based on the Ford Escort

RIGHT BELOW The delightful Ghia Brezza was a sports coupé powered by a mid-mounted 1.6 litre Ford engine

BELOW This elegant reworking of the MkII Ford Granada was known as the Ghia Altair

for the Maserati Ghibli and Indy, as well as Panteras for the European market, Ernesto Guarienco, who looks after final preparation of Ghia prototypes, was giving the sleekly rounded Brezza a final inspection before pronouncing it ready for the road.

Italian racing *rosso chiaro* (bright red), the mid-engined Brezza was powered by a 1.6 litre CVH unit from the North American EXP two-seater sports derivative of the Escort, using an automatic transmission to ease the task of connecting the gear linkage when the engine of the Escort was used to drive the back wheels instead of the front. Spatted rear wheels and flying buttresses over the engine cover made the Brezza look like a baby Ferrari.

Filippo taped a battered *Prova* trade plate on Brezza's immaculate red rump, got in and started the car; I climbed into the passenger seat and we drove off down the deeply rutted via Egeo, which faces the Ghia plant. At its head, Filippo nonchalantly launched the Brezza into the thick of Turin's mid-afternoon traffic that was rushing down the Corso Dante as furiously as only Italian traffic can. In a couple of weeks the Brezza was to star in the Turin Show; now it was just proving its worth as a car amid the tiny Fiats that were jockeying for position in the traffic light grand prix, swooping perilously close to the Brezza so that their drivers could take a closer look.

We drove the car round the block, then pulled on to a cycle track outside

ABOVE A concept for an urban sports car, the Ghia Shuttler was based on a shortened Fiesta floorplan

LEFT ABOVE Despite its compact dimensions, the Ghia Pockar city car could seat five. Its Fiesta engine was moved to the rear of the car, while there were special lockable luggage compartments in either door

LEFT BELOW The compact dimensions of the Shuttler made it exceptionally easy to park in confined spaces

the local park to take some photographs. Two rows of bare trees converged into the afternoon mist as I photographed the Brezza. Suddenly, I became aware of a change in the background noise: the mob of kids—the Torinese *raggazzi*—who had been playing a rowdy game of football in the park had stopped, and were crowding the park railings alongside the Brezza. Unable to climb over, they stretched out their arms as if to try and touch the sleek little car.

'*O bella!*' they chorused. '*Che bella machina!*'

That's the secret of Ghia: its showcars really work, can really be driven. They're not just inanimate, soulless dummies moulded from fibreglass: you can actually prove the value of a concept in its true element, the road.

One recurring theme at Ghia has been the development of city cars with a touch of style, a hint of urban elegance, like the 1980 Pockar, a five-seater built on a dramatically shortened Fiesta platform, with the powertrain moved to the rear. What it had lost in length, the Pockar recovered in height, several years before the Japanese began building taller urban vehicles. Moreover, there was no loss in luggage accommodation, thanks to lockable external com-

LEFT ABOVE Rear view of the Ghia Cockpit, powered by a rear-mounted Piaggio engine

LEFT BELOW The Trio city car was a 1980s reworking of the bubble car idea that was so popular in the 1950s

ABOVE Access to the tandem-seated
interior of the Cockpit is by raising
the counterbalanced canopy

partments in either door, supplemented by a stowage tray across the inside of the windscreen and a package tray over the rear engine.

Then there was the Shuttler, built a couple of years later, which I drove in Brussels in the depths of winter just before the car was due to go into the Brussels Salon. Again, a shortened Fiesta platform was used, but this time the aim was to create a sporty two-seater that was compact enough for the most congested city centre, yet had adequate performance for out-of-town motoring.

Driving among the Bruxellois trams and parking in quite impossibly small spaces, the Shuttler fully proved the validity of its design: and when, a couple of years later, it went on display in the French National Automobile Museum in Mulhouse, its shape still looked futuristic, even though a new generation of aerodynamic production cars like the Sierra had appeared in the interval.

Another theme that Ghia has followed in show vehicles is that of the 'people mover', what the industry calls the 'high cube' vehicle, in which, by building tall, you can increase the amount of passenger accommodation within a given wheelbase. Such a vehicle was the APV—the initials stand

ABOVE Access to the tandem-seated interior of the Cockpit is by raising the counterbalanced canopy

LEFT BELOW The wooden hammer form over which the Ghia panel-beaters formed the AC-Ghia's bodywork

LEFT ABOVE The AC-Ghia was a stunning reworking of the square-cut AC ME3000; it revived the traditional tie-up between Ford and AC that had flourished in the days of the Cobra

ABOVE Also based on the mid-engined AC ME3000 chassis, the Quicksilver was remarkable in being a mid-engined four-door five-seater

for 'All Purpose Vehicle'—which could carry seven passengers (or a phenomenal amount of luggage) within the wheelbase of an Escort Estate.

I arranged for APV to be shown in the British Design Council's 'Drive Forward' exhibition during 1984, which was opened in London by the Prime Minister, Mrs Margaret Thatcher. She, I fear, felt that the bonnet line fell away too sharply, even though it contributed to excellent forward visibility and a very low drag factor, and argued that she liked to be able to see the further corners of a car from the driving seat.

Her parting shot to us, which was gleefully picked up and used out of context by the press, was: 'You'll have to redesign it for me!'

The British press the next day was full of headlines of the 'Thatcher criticizes new Ford' variety; we could hardly complain about the breadth of coverage given by the APV, and in any case, it underlined perfectly the fact that a prime purpose of a show car is to act as a sounding board for public opinion, even when that public happens to be the greatest Commoner!

In any history of successful showcars, there's room for the odd eccentricity created to draw the crowds through the sheer perversity of its design. And so in the 1980s Ghia created Cockpit and Trio. The Cockpit concept revisited the old sporting threewheeler layout made famous in the heroic days of motoring by the Morgan trike, with the idea of 'providing regular intercity highway transportation in a period of severe energy crisis'. If, in the event, Cockpit had more of the post-Suez Messerschmitt than the Morgan Super Sports about it, nevertheless, it remains an attractive little vehicle.

Its two passengers sit in tandem under a glazed plastic canopy like the cockpit hood of a fighter plane. Hinged at the front, the whole canopy and the laminated glass windscreen lift up on hydraulic struts. Power is by an air-cooled single-cylinder Piaggio 200 cc scooter engine, driving the single rear wheel though a four-speed transmission with quadrant change; a somewhat breathless reverse is provided by running the electric starting motor backwards.

Though it's fairly low-powered, Cockpit is still capable of quite rapid motoring—I have vivid memories of Ford of Europe chairman, Bob Lutz,

Developed to show a modern interpretation of the traditional sports two-seater theme, the Fiesta XR2-based Barchetta provoked widespread enthusiasm—and demands that it should be put into production

lapping Dunton's test track high on the banking with the Piaggio engine revving hard, no easy feat with a three-wheeler, for the middle wheel tends to hop down the banked track. And afterwards, we tried to devise what a 'Super-Cockpit', with a bigger engine and larger, wider-tracked wheels, would look like. . . .

As for Trio, that's a delightfully odd city car, based on the powertrain of one of those curious little delivery trikes that are so popular in Italy. The engine and continuously variable belt drive were mounted at the back of a specially-built four-wheeled tubular chassis, whose front track was considerably narrower than the back. It carried rounded three-seater bodywork, whose resemblance to an Easter Egg was accentuated by its chocolate brown colour scheme: its seating capacity was achieved by mounting the seats in arrowhead formation, with the driver in the centre, ahead of the two passengers.

The Trio, which was sent to the United States, was remarkable for the weight-saving techniques practised in its construction, which included a floor made from a honeycomb sandwich of aluminium and fibreglass and windows made of metacrylate, a scratchproof plastic stronger, yet lighter, than glass. Kerb weight was only just over 6.6 cwt.

The 1980s have seen a flowering of Ghia showcars such as has not been seen since the heady days of the early 1950s, exciting cars that could maybe, someday, have real production potential. Cars like the AC-Ghia, an outstanding two-seater sports coupé based on the chassis of the AC ME3000, an aggressive-looking two-seater powered by a mid-mounted Ford 3-litre Essex V6 engine.

Where the original ME3000 is uncompromisingly square-cut, the AC-Ghia has soft, flowing lines that have won universal praise: moreover, since it's built on a fully-developed sports car chassis, AC-Ghia is road-ready without any of the allowances that have to be made for the average show car built on an ordinary family car chassis. It's a design that has, since it was launched at the 1981 Geneva Show, continued to cause excitement and fuel speculation that one day it might be put into production, not necessarily by Ford.

The car that Mrs Thatcher wanted redesigned—the Ghia APV seven-seater

The AC-Ghia theme was further developed in the Quicksilver, one of the very few five-seat, four-door sports saloons to be built on a mid-engined chassis. Though the AC ME3000 platform was once again used, this time the wheelbase had been increased by some 11.4 in to 9 ft 8 in. to accommodate the longer bodywork. And despite the aerodynamic bodywork and mid-engine configuration, not only were all the passengers housed within the wheelbase, but there was also a creditable 124 cu. ft of luggage accommodation. Like the AC-Ghia, it's a design that might one day go into production under licence.

Another unusual four-door saloon car built by Ghia was Probe IV, unveiled at the Detroit Automobile Show in January 1983. Designed and engineered by Ford's International Design Centre in Dearborn, Probe IV was transformed into a fully-functional car by the unique skills of Ghia; it was a race against the clock to get the Probe completed on time, for it was due to be airfreighted out of Turin on Christmas Eve, 1982, and I recall that the deadline was so tight that while the super-streamlined car was pushed across the road to be weighed for the shippers on the OSI weighbridge, one of the Ghia craftsmen was applying the decorative red side tape striping as he was walking alongside the moving Probe!

In America, Probe IV, which took streamlining to the extent not only of full flush glazing but also front wheels faired in behind flexible skirts and computer-controlled suspension that varied the car's angle of attack according to its speed, was tested in the Lockheed windtunnel at Marietta, Georgia, and recorded a drag coefficient of only 0.15—equivalent, apparently, to that of a jet fighter 'plane. . . .

While I was gathering material for the press release on Probe IV, I wandered round the Ghia workshops, a marvellous secret place only accessible to accredited personnel. It's there that the Ghia panelbeaters practice their incredible skills, forming metal with a dexterity that has to be seen to be believed. A very special design exercise was taking shape, a personal dream of Bob Lutz.

Mounted on trestles was an XR2 chassis; alongside was a wood and plaster mockup of a stubby two-seater sports car with exciting lines. A panelbeater was shaping a panel over a wooden former in just the same way that, half a millenium earlier, his ancestors would have shaped a suit of armour over a baulk of timber. As if by magic, the metal took on independent life, became a fulsomely rounded panel. 'Yes,' said Sapino, 'the car will be beautiful. We call it the Barchetta. But it will never be shown.'

Barchetta, it seems was going to be one of the 20 or so Ghia prototypes built every year that are never publicly exhibited. These tangible dreams that are helping to form the cars of the day after tomorrow are only shown to a select and critical audience of the most senior executives at Ford. They range from static full-scale models of the new car of four or five years hence to functional, handbuilt prototypes that can be assessed in the secure environment of a Ford test track. Born to bloom unseen, they will probably be broken up when they have served their purpose.

But all the motoring enthusiasts at Ford who saw the finished Barchetta felt that it was too good to be condemned to this covert existence, that it deserved a wider audience who would judge it on its merits, to see whether this 'affordable and attractive two-seater convertible using modern front-wheel-drive powertrain and chassis components' was worthy to be recommended for future production.

And in the autumn of 1983, against all odds, Barchetta made its debut before the public at the Frankfurt Motor Show. Since then, it has been exhibited on both sides of the Atlantic, always to an enthusiastic reception. Typical was the reaction of America's *Car and Driver*: 'The Barchetta is potentially the best combination of sports-car zip and econocar sip since the MG TC.'

But how did Barchetta make that dramatic step into the spotlight—and why? I asked Bob Lutz: 'The Barchetta was born (conceptually) at the Geneva Show in March 1982 when Karl Ludvigsen and I wandered around, deploring the lack of a modern, low-cost two-seater,' he recalled. 'We got talking to Eric Bitter, of Bitter Cars, and, over a glass or two, agreed that there had to be sufficient potential for a latter-day MG TC or, really, reincarnated Porsche Speedster—no options, side-curtains, flop-hood. . . .'

'We also agreed that it had to have an *unmodified* high-volume platform: the desire by the designers to "just take the engine and move the whole powertrain behind the seats—no trouble at all" was to be resisted at all costs. Karl said he would take it on, get an XR2 chassis, and talk to Filippo and Don Kopka. That's how it got going.'

'I gave it the name, because "Barchetta" ("little boat" or "skiff") is what the Italians traditionally called spartan high-performance roadsters—the kind that ran in the Mille Miglia—there were Lancia barchettas, Ferrari barchettas and even Fiat, too.'

But Bob, who was then vice president of Ford's International Automotive Operations, found that, exciting though the Barchetta concept was, it was frustratingly impossible to engender the same enthusiasm for the project with the then Ford of Europe management, who were unable to identify the low-cost/low-investment manufacturing source that Barchetta needed to become viable. So he decided to show the car publicly: 'I thought we might as well get some value out of showing it—and maybe whet sufficient appetites to get a programme going after all.'

Mid-1984 saw another step for Ghia, with the revival of the Vignale name on an aerodynamic four-wheel drive concept car, the Ghia Vignale Mustang. With flush glass, smoothly contoured windscreen with single wiper, low profile aerodynamic headlamps and partial belly pan, the Ghia Vignale Mustang was equipped with a Ferguson Formula permanently-engaged four-wheel-drive conversion with viscous-coupling automatic limited slip differential and powered by the latest 2.3 litre Ford SVO turbocharged overhead cam four-cylinder power point. A dramatically handsome car, it too, attracted eulogies from the enthusiast motoring press.

In November 1984, the Ghia plant was chosen as the venue for the public unveiling of Ford's exciting RS200 rally car, whose chunky two-seater coupé body had been designed by Ghia.

In an unbelievably short space of time, the main hall of Ghia, where Ghiblis and Panteras had once been built, was transformed into a conference centre, complete with a small museum of Ghia prototypes and production cars, where journalists from all over Europe had their first sight of the RS200 and of the TSX-4, a neat and beautifully-finished estate car based on the American Ford Tempo platform. Included in the TSX-4's equipment were a television to entertain the rear seat passengers, a portable computer in the passenger's glovebox, and a compact disc player; interior trim was in sensuously soft grey leather, with contrast red decorative slashing in seat bases and backs.

As for the RS200, with its ingenious optional four- or two-wheel drive and a potent mid-mounted turbocharged twin-cam power unit, it stole the Turin Show from under the noses of the Italian manufacturers, proving that, only a few months short of its seventieth birthday, Ghia had lost none of the design skill and flair for creating *carrozzerie di gran lusso e di gran sport* that had first brought the company's products into the public eye!

An early Ghia design rendering for the Ford RS200 rally car project

7 Ghia the world over

When it comes to mainstream Fords, the Ghia designation is synonymous with top-of-the-line luxury. Obviously, Ghia doesn't build these luxurious derivatives of the standard Ford range in its Turin plant, for Ghia never made that giant step to become an 'industrialized' coachbuilder. But when every new model range is planned, Ghia is part of the design process right from the beginning, producing concepts which are considered along with the work of Ford's other European design studios, in Dunton, England, and Merkenich, Germany.

The ideas of its designers are a vital component of the design process, and when it comes to specifying trim and equipment for the luxury models that are to bear the Ghia name, the Turin studio submits a number of proposals which are used as the basis for the eventual production version. Right from the start of Ford's use of the Ghia name on its production models, the keynote has been 'detail refinement'—which back in 1974 Bill Bourke called 'the bespoke tailoring, haute couture touch'.

Around the world, the following selected Ford models have borne the Ghia designation:

Europe

The first European Ghia-badged Fords were the Granada Ghia and Capri Ghia launched in February 1974, followed that July by the fastback Granada Ghia Coupe. Of the Granada Ghia, Filippo Sapino remarked: 'The only way to make a luxury car is in refined good taste, and that has been our criterion. You achieve this optically by the styling, colour balance and texture used, and in a more detailed way by the quality of materials and craftsmanship of construction.'

In January 1975, a Ghia version of the Mark II Escort was launched, followed a year later by the Mk IV Taunus Ghia in Germany. In Britain, the Cortina Ghia appeared in September 1976 when the Mk IV Cortina range was introduced; there were both saloon and estate car versions. Obviously, given Turin's contribution to the Fiesta programme, there had to be a Fiesta Ghia, which duly made its appearance in June 1976 in Germany, and in February 1977 in Britain. When the all-new front-wheel-drive Escort was launched in September 1980, there was naturally a Ghia variant of that car, too.

LEFT Europe's first Ghia model Ford was the 1974 Granada Ghia, with its distinctive radiator grille

BELOW LEFT The interior of the Granada Ghia was styled in Turin, too

LEFT The Granada Ghia concept
moves on a generation—this was the
Mark II version of the car in 1982

BELOW And this was its side
elevation; note the distinctive Ghia-
styled alloy wheels

ABOVE The first Escort Ghia
appeared on the Mark II range in
1978

FAR LEFT ABOVE The original 1973
Capri Ghia, photographed outside
the Borgo Medievale in Turin

FAR LEFT BELOW Rear view of the
1978 Capri II Ghia

CENTRE This is the 1976 Taunus/
Cortina Ghia, again, the first Ghia
version of this model line

BELOW Rear view of the 1976
Taunus 2.3 Ghia

ABOVE The Ghia Escort was introduced in 1980

FAR LEFT ABOVE Ghia designs had formed a strong influence on the shape of the 1976 Fiesta; appropriately, this minicar range has had a Ghia variant from the start of production

FAR LEFT BELOW This is the latest version of the Fiesta Ghia, launched in late 1983

LEFT Rear view of the 1980 Escort Ghia 1.6

173

ABOVE An unusual Ghia model, the luxurious Transit Ghia bus, in its 1984 form, powered by the economical 2.5 DI diesel

LEFT The Ghia version of the Ford Sierra was launched at the end of 1982

More recent Ghia-badged European Fords have been the Ghia Transit, a station wagon developed from the popular Ford van and sold only in Continental Europe, the Sierra (introduced in September 1982) and the Orion, launched at the end of 1983, whose Ghia version is available either with a standard 1600 cc Ford CVH engine developing 79 bhp or with its potent fuel-injection derivative which has a power output of 105 bhp. Latest Ford model with a Ghia version is the Scorpio, the new large luxury car launched in the spring of 1985, and sold in Britain as 'Granada'.

European Ford's latest is the Scorpio/Granada Ghia—a truly luxury car, at last

South Africa

Ford's South African subsidiary has, for the most part, followed Europe with its Ghia models, which have included the Granada Ghia (July 1974), Mk IV Cortina Ghia (July 1980) and the Ghia version of the new Granada (January 1981).

But in January 1975, Ford South Africa announced a model created in a limited edition of only 200 units, the Burgundy Ghia, which had 'unique red velvet metallic paint, Beaumont Cloud cloth trim and a unique red odense vinyl roof which is colour-keyed to the car'. Every purchaser was given a special colour-keyed wallet and keyring, plus a certificate denoting the build number of the car; he could also have his monogram in stick-on metal letters affixed to the front door of the car.

North America

In August 1973, Ford announced the Mustang II range: the tangled design history of the Mustang II Ghia was fudged in a press release which merely said that the model was 'a super luxury notchback model named after Ford's Italian design studio'.

For 1975, the Granada (which had nothing in common with its European namesake) and the Mercury Monarch were available in Ghia guise, their interiors 'evoking the touch of a refined cabinetmaker': Ford Canada described the cars as *les plus somptueux* in its French-language release.

ABOVE The South African 2.0 litre Cortina Ghia, dating from January 1981

FAR LEFT ABOVE A unique model for South Africa, the Granada Burgundy Ghia, introduced in March 1975

FAR LEFT BELOW This is South Africa's version of the Cortina Ghia, launched in 1979

LEFT Like other South African Ghia models, this 1981 Granada Ghia differs in trim details from its European counterparts

ABOVE This was Canada's version of the Mustang II, which appeared in the Dominion's dealerships on 21 September, 1973

FAR LEFT ABOVE This South African version of the Granada Ghia, dating from November 1982, was powered by the 3 litre Essex V6 engine, while the European equivalent had a 2.8 litre V6

LEFT The 1975 Canadian Mustang II had revised styling, including a 'silver half-vinyl roof and cranberry interior'

ABOVE 'The chic and distinguished
interior of the 1975 Granada and
Monarch,' claimed Ford-Granada,
'evokes the touch of a refined
cabinet-maker in the most
sumptuous Ghia models . . .'

RIGHT Canada's 1975 Granada Ghia
had nothing but the name in
common with its European
counterpart

Mustang II Ghia gained an 'opera window' as an 'exclusive feature', which must have alleviated to some extent the massive blind spot caused by the dummy vinyl-covered hood which in the 'Silver Luxury Ghia' was colour-matched to the metallic silver paintwork. . . . With the launch of the restyled Mustang range, a hatchback variant of the Ghia was also available.

For 1980, a Ghia version of the Fairmont was added to the lineup. It had only its name in common with the Australian Fairmont, but by 1981, the Ghia name was once again restricted to the Mustang range, and dropped even from this the following year.

Australia

The first Australian-built Ford to bear the Ghia name was the Mk II Escort, followed a couple of years later by the Mk IV Cortina. In 1980, a Fairmont Ghia was also added, which in Australian guise looked very like the European Granada, though it was powered by a 4.1 litre straight six. For 1982, the Fairmont gained a restyled front end.

In 1981, Ford Australia launched its Laser series, developed in conjunction with Mazda, in which Ford had a 25 per cent stake: the range was compatible with the European Escort, though the powertrain was identical to that of the Mazda 323. Both saloon and station wagon Ghia versions were offered.

When the Mazda 626-powered Telstar range replaced the Cortina in Ford Australia's line-up for 1984, Ghia sedan and hatchbacks were included in the line-up.

Argentina

Ford Argentina built the Mk III Taunus long after the model had been phased out in Europe: in 1982, the European Mk IV began to be assembled by Ford Argentina. To differentiate it from the old Taunus, which was still being offered, Ford Argentina only offered the new model in its Ghia incarnation, with the North American 'Pinto' in-line 2.3 litre straight-four engine.

The following year, the Argentinian Taunus Ghia appeared in 'S' form as well, with a fastback two-door coupé body that was unique to the Argentinian market: the Taunus Ghia S coupé lasted only one year, after which the coupé body was only available on the GT or its garish 'SP' derivative.

And for 1984, a Ghia version of the Argentinian Falcon line was announced, powered by a 3.6 litre in-line six, available in two stages of tune, giving a top speed of 97 mph in standard form, 112 mph in 'SP' guise.

Another early joint venture between Turin and Dearborn, the Mercury Monarch Ghia of 1973 was somewhat lacking in *elan*

Appendix

GHIA'S ALTER EGO—VIGNALE

The display of the elegant Ghia Vignale Mustang on the Ghia stand at the 1984 Turin Motor Show marked the reappearance of one of the city's more famous coachbuilding names after a ten-year gap. Vignale had closed down in 1974 as a result of the dramatic fall-off in the Pantera market: the reintroduction of that distinctive badge bearing Turin's famous landmark, the dome and tall spire of the 'Mole Antonelliana', between the arms of the letter 'V' could herald the birth of a new series of sporting Ford prototypes. . . .

The firm's founder, Alfredo Vignale, was born in Turin in 1913, the fourth of seven children. By the time he was 11, Alfredo was already working in metal, and at the age of 17, he joined Stabilimenti Farina as a sheet metal worker.

After the war, Vignale and his partner Balma Angelo opened a little workshop in 1946 as a prelude to his ambition of the establishment of a proper *carrozzeria*.

Simultaneously, Vignale was working for Cisitalia, for whom he produced three aerodynamic coupés which pioneered the 'porthole' styling feature in the front wings, which was quickly copied by Buick. He also created a streamlined body on a Fiat 500 chassis which was widely admired—but credited to another coachbuilder! The resultant apology in the press helped to spread Vignale's fame, and in 1948 he was able to establish his own *carrozzeria*.

That year, his Fiat 1500 Spyder won the Grand Prix d'Europe at Juan les Pins; at first he specialized in coachwork for Fiat and Lancia chassis, but his reputation was really founded on an order for a special coupé on an early Ferrari chassis belonging to the Princess Liliana de Rethy.

That was followed by commissions to body the cars of Ferrari's works sports car team; Vignale-bodied Ferraris won three Mille Miglia and the Carrera Panamerica Mexico in the period 1950–53.

During that time, Vignale produced over 100 bodies for Ferrari chassis as well as special Fiats and Lancias; most of the designs were by the freelance Giovanni Michelotti. He developed a remarkable rapport with Vignale, who could translate Michelotti's drawings directly into metal without an intermediate fullsize 'buck'. Consequently, all of Vignale's cars were a touch assymmetrical. . . .

After 1953, the links with Ferrari were broken as Pinin Farina established

an alliance with the Modenese firm, but Vignale continued to progress; in 1957 they built a Michelotti-designed streamlined coupé body for a Fiat Abarth 750. The aerodynamics were so good that this 750 cc, 47 bhp car could touch 100 mph.

At this time, Vignale was making the transition from one-off production to 'small series', which meant that the company outgrew its premises on the via Cigliano, and moved into a large modern factory at Grugliasco, not far from Fiat's Mirafiori works. A further consequence of the increase in output was a changeover from aluminium to steel for the body panelling.

By now, Vignale was working with Maserati, starting with the 3500GT Cabriolet, of which 242 were produced; simultaneously, the firm was building coupé and convertible bodies for the Fiat 600/750. This was succeeded by a series of special bodies—saloon, coupé and spyder—for the Fiat 850, plus a sport coupé based on the Fiat 124. Alongside these, the relationship with Maserati blossomed: the Sebring was announced in 1963, the Mexico in 1965. The Mexico, however, was outsold by Ghia's Ghibli, with production only reaching 250 units, but its successor, the Indy, achieved total worldwide sales of 1136 cars.

Bodies were also produced for the English Jensen, though Vignale's name was perhaps more closely identified in Britain with the Standard Vignale Vanguard, which was no more than a mild 'Italian job' in styling terms.

Vignale's bread and butter had been reclothed versions of lower-priced mass-production models, particularly Fiat; when these adopted unitary construction, the job became much more expensive, with a consequent sharp fall in orders, resulting in a financial crisis.

At this point, Alejandro de Tomaso stepped in and snapped up Vignale as a production facility for the Pantera; three days after the sale, Alfredo Vignale was dead in that inexplicable car crash.

ABOVE Vignale's stand at the 1966 Turin Show includes Fiat, Jensen and Maserati designs; the juxtaposition of the Ghia badge is a portent of things to come

RIGHT The four-wheel-drive Ghia Vignale Mustang of 1984 was the first car to bear the Vignale name for a decade

ABOVE This varied line-up of Frua-
bodied Fiat 1100s was photographed
in 1954

TOP This design for a sports car was exhibited at Turin in 1984 by Tom Tjaarda's new company, Dimensione Design

ABOVE Frua's Maserati Gran Sport dates from 1954; its bodywork could have been manufactured in the Ghia shops

THE GHIA CONNECTION

The influence of Ghia on the Italian coachbuilding industry has been immense; many of the best-known designers of the past 30 years have, at some time, worked with—or for—Carrozzeria Ghia.

Apart from the work he carried out for Fiat after resigning from Ghia in 1953, Felice Mario Boano also bodied more exalted marques. One of his earliest ventures in this direction was an ultra-streamlined two-seater coupé on the Jaguar XK140C—the 210 hp 'special equipment' version of the XK140 with C-type cylinder head—built in conjunction with the American designer Raymond Loewy in 1955.

The two men, said *The Autocar*, 'had striven to get the best of both worlds: performance and silence. Wherever possible, sound-deadening materials were used and the shape of the car was specifically intended to reduce noise to the minimum and ensure the maximum stability.'

At the following year's Turin Show, Boano exhibited a sleek coupé on an Alfa Romeo 1900 chassis: the press remarked on its slim pillars—and on its somewhat surprising pink and black colour scheme. 'The hood,' noted *The Autocar*, 'is a pink nylon cloth, beautifully woven....'

At the beginning of 1985, Felice Mario Boano was living in retirement not far from Turin.

The involvement of Pietro Frua with Ghia is far less clear-cut: he certainly designed a number of cars for them, but there are indications that some of Frua's designs were built by Ghia: certainly several photos of Frua-bodied Maseratis and Fiats appear in the Ghia photographic files, though I found no proof one way or the other to confirm this theory in the Ghia archives (which largely consist of invoices retained for the benefit of the Italian state

A second variation on the Maserati Gran Sport by Frua, this time built in 1956

Photographed at a 1947 concours
d'elegance in Turin, this Lancia
Astura bears an early Frua body; was
this one built by Ghia?

fiscal police). But it would go a long way to explain that dispute over the origins of the Renault Floride. . . .

Frua's contemporary as a freelance designer with Ghia, Michelotti (who also worked for Ghia-Aigle) is, of course, best known to Britons for his work with Standard-Triumph, and for his ultimate design, the Reliant SS, a slightly odd-looking two-seater sports car which hit the market shortly after Michelotti's death in 1984.

Tom Tjaarda is still working in Turin, over a quarter of a century after that young architecture student from Detroit was invited to join Ghia on a temporary basis by Segre. After he left Ghia, Tom worked at Pininfarina, then joined the Fiat Design Centre. He next moved on to Rayton Fissore, where he designed the Saab Viking sports, the Rona and Magnum 4 × 4 projects.

Most recently, he has founded his own design centre, 'Dimensione Design', whose projects range from automotive models to electronic and information machines, from consumer and commercial projects to home and boutique furnishings. His portfolio includes steering wheels and seats for Ferrero, electronic equipment for Urmet, wheels for Fergat, a helicopter for Silvercraft and a complete chain of boutiques for Pratesi. And his latest automotive project is a two-seater sports car, shown in model form at the 1984 Turin Show.

But of all the 'alumni' of Ghia, Giorgetto Giugiaro is the best-known, for his Turin-based design house, Ital Design, acts as consultant to all the

leading car companies and created such models as the Fiat Uno, the Lotus
Etna, the Alfasud and the Saab 9000 Turbo (and, on the debit side, the
Morris Ital); he has also designed watches for Seiko, cameras for Nikon,
motorcycles for Suzuki and is currently launching a range of 'technical,
rational and functional' menswear under the 'Giugiaro Uomo' name. This
multi-talented designer—remarkably, still only in his mid-40s—has also
created a new form of pasta, grooved to retain the sauce. . . .

At the 1984 Turin Show, I asked Giugiaro what he remembered of his
days with Ghia: 'The ambience was really exciting. I was free to take my
decisions on designs and work programmes for the styling department and
prototype workshop. The results were seen at the 1966 Turin Motor Show
when—with a really record performance—Ghia presented four good
novelties: the Maserati Ghibli, the Mangusta, the Fiat 850 Vanessa and the
De Tomaso Pampero.

'I was a really good friend of Gaspardo Moro, who tended to leave me
free to operate. My decision to leave Ghia was due to De Tomaso's arrival
at the firm: he made autonomous design management impossible.

'However, in order to keep faith with my contract with Ghia, I remained
as a consultant from 1967 to 1968, when I founded Ital Design. The Ghia
team of modellers and workers consisted of really professional people, so
I was able to persuade a good number of my colleagues to follow me to
Ital Design when I decided to found my own company.

'While I was at Ghia, I worked on the following projects: Ghia 450SS,
Isuzu 117 Coupé, De Tomaso 2000 Competizione, De Tomaso Pampero,
De Tomaso Mangusta, Maserati Ghibli, Fiat 850 Vanessa, Fiat Dino Coupé,
Iso Rivolta Fidia, Oldsmobile Toronado Thor, Rowan Elettrica, De Tomaso
Mangusta Spider and Maserati Simun.

'Of those, the only cars I designed that I'm sorry I don't own are the
Ghibli and the Mangusta.'

The attribution of this splendidly
adipose Alfa Romeo Roadster of
1947 is curious in the extreme: on
the back of the photo is written 'Alfa
Romeo Farina Frua'. Was this
another Frua sub-contract job? And
why is the photo in the Ghia
archives? It can't be just for the
lady's legs . . .

Index